ONCE TO EVERY MAN AND NATION

ONCE TO EVERY MAN AND NATION

*Stories about becoming
a Bahá'í*

edited by

Randie and Steven Gottlieb

GEORGE RONALD
OXFORD

GEORGE RONALD, Publisher
46 High Street, Kidlington, Oxford OX5 2DN

'Every Friday Night' © Priscilla J. Triplett

British Library Cataloguing in Publication Data

Gottlieb, Randie
   Once to every man and nation : stories about becoming a Bahá'í.
   I. Title   II. Gottlieb, Steven
   297'.8944   BP365

   ISBN 0-85398-211-2 Pbk

Set by Quad Left Typesetting in 11 on 13 point
Printed in England

Contents

Special Thanks

To all the authors
who so generously contributed their stories

and

to Carolyn Hansen
who collected and typed a number
of the manuscripts

To Marc, Rory, Stacey, Dennie, and Deb

Preface

Once to Every Man and Nation is a collection of stories by thirty-seven individuals describing how each became a Bahá'í. Its purpose is to record those moving and memorable personal accounts that we so often hear at Bahá'í gatherings, and which we share informally with one another. These autobiographical sketches are intended to assist and confirm Bahá'ís in their teaching efforts, while those who are investigating the Bahá'í Faith may find stories which particularly reflect their own experiences and concerns.

The collection contains a wide variety of accounts, from straightforward investigation and acceptance of the Bahá'í teachings to the unlikely coincidences and unusual events which sometimes occur. In one story a young man, thinking he is going to a marshmallow roast, attends his first Bahá'í meeting and is overwhelmed by the love and spirituality of the Bahá'ís. In another, a pregnant woman, believing she is about to die, sees a saintly figure in a red robe and searches for the meaning of her vision.

In limiting itself to North America, *Once to Every Man and Nation* nevertheless reflects a great diversity of cultural, racial and social backgrounds and demonstrates that there is no *one* type of person who is attracted to the Bahá'í Faith. (A second volume of stories from all over the world is now in preparation.) Although there seems to be no single pattern of investigation, the patience, warmth and perseverance of the Bahá'í teachers stand out again and again. We hope you enjoy reading these stories as much as we have.

The editors
October 1985

Marshmallow Roast

by John R. Rushford

A friend of mine said, 'John, you seem like a thinker. Why don't you come to a fireside with me?' 'Okay,' I replied, 'but not tonight. Maybe next week.' Next week came and I was all prepared, thinking I was going to a fireside — maybe roast marshmallows or something. You see, I lived in St. Thomas, Virgin Islands. It's very warm there, but in the winter season you could easily have a fire, especially if you lived high up. Anyway, I was prepared to go to a fireside.

We walked about three streets out of town to the Bahá'í Center. Upon entering, I saw an old friend who used to be my drinking partner. We laughed, talked, had coffee, and waited for others to arrive. Well, they did, and here I was, sitting around talking about God. I will never forget the faces of those people: a native lady, two very attractive girls and some great guys who all believed in God, but who were not extreme in dress or personal belief. What I am trying to say is, here were these lovely people sitting around in a circle, and I received such love from them. They believed in and loved God, but were 'real' people. They told me that our true reality was spiritual, and that we were created to know God and to love Him. It made me think.

After about ten firesides (informal talks where many of my questions were answered and books were offered), they invited me to a Riḍván observance. It was in a lovely garden, and leading the singing was another of these wonderful people, so full of the love of God, you could feel it. There were about twenty people at this gathering, and all welcomed me with friendship, love, and brotherhood.

1

Before I met the Bahá'ís, I didn't know the true meaning of religion. The Bahá'ís had it. I enrolled at the next Feast.

The Figure in the Red Robe

by Roma M. Freeman

We were expecting our third child, due in May of 1956. It had been an extremely difficult pregnancy from beginning to end. At the same time, I was suffering with a broken rib and pneumonia, and every cough racked my body with pain. On the twentieth of March, almost two months early, severe labor pains began to develop. I thrashed about the bed, whipping from side to side, turning, twisting, thinking and verbalizing many thoughts that were far, far from lofty or noble.

All of a sudden to the right of the bed, approximately five feet away, there appeared a male figure clad in a floor-length deep red robe. His beautiful hands were opened and extended towards me. He had a black, neatly-groomed beard and black shoulder-length hair that produced red highlights in the sunlight streaming through the bedroom window. His eyes were gentle, filled with love and compassion, yet those same eyes seemed to register such disappointment and sorrow, as he witnessed the behavior I was exhibiting.

At that moment, I felt such shame and yet such fright! Who was he? What was he doing here? He reminded me of the statues and paintings I had seen of Jesus Christ, but I knew it wasn't Jesus. Maybe it was Saint Peter? But how could that be? I doubted the existence of God and no longer believed in the station of Jesus, much less in a Saint Peter. But here he was, whoever he was, standing near my bed in human form. I was so frightened! It had to mean that I was losing my mind, or that I was going to die and would soon meet him again at the pearly gates — or at least meet him on the way by the pearly gates to some other place. I quickly turned my head away from those eyes and those beautiful hands. When I turned back to look again, he was gone. I began to cry uncontrollably. Oh God, what did all this mean?

There was no one I could ask. What would they think? Perhaps they would believe that I was losing touch with reality, or hallucinating because of the many months of pain and difficulty. But I knew in my heart that it was real! It was true. Yet I had never, never believed such things. I had always scoffed at those who mentioned such experiences, which I viewed as figments of the imagination.

After our baby was born, I did share the experience with my Aunt Mae. I had always been able to share anything with her. She would understand, and would respond honestly. But this she could neither explain nor understand. So for many years I searched museums, galleries, libraries, book stores, everywhere, with the hope of seeing that face again and perhaps discovering who it was. Although the unsuccessful search was finally abandoned, the hope still remained. His face was one I could never forget.

In 1957, while serving on the Cape Cod Council for the Massachusetts Commission Against Discrimination, I met Ethelinda and Harry Merson of Falmouth, Massachusetts. They were very unusual people. They always seemed so positive and sincere in their approach to the various racial problems presented to the Committee. I was impressed, yet doubtful and suspicious too. It was rare, if ever, for me to be impressed by the sincerity of any Caucasian. This was disturbing. I shared my feelings with the chairman of the Committee and questioned why the Mersons were so different. The chairman explained that Harry was Superintendent of Falmouth Schools and that Ethelinda was his wife. I knew this had nothing to do with what I saw and felt about them. It was also mentioned that both were Bahá'ís. This was a strange word which meant nothing, as I had never heard it before. On returning home, I consulted an encyclopedia to determine what this Bahá'í was all about. Upon discovering that it was an organized religion, that was enough. I had discovered all I wanted to know.

In 1960, a friend mentioned that if she ever were to belong to any religion, it would be Bahá'í. Here was that strange word again. She wrote to Wilmette, Illinois, the Bahá'í National Center, for some literature. I read it, and again, that was enough of that!

Later in the sixties, another friend, who was investigating the Bahá'í Faith, excitedly encouraged me to read a few books written by Hand of the Cause of God, Mr. William Sears. Mr. Sears had been a radio announcer in our home town and he also just happened to be a Bahá'í. Here was that word again!

In 1966, while visiting Toronto, Canada, I was given a Bahá'í prayer book, *The Divine Art of Living*, and *Bahá'u'lláh and the New Era*, by one of the new friends I had met there. As this was a critical juncture in my life and some difficult decisions had to be made, my friend thought these books might help. This I doubted, but what did I have to lose? So I read them and found that each book sparked a great deal of intellectual curiosity. Who was this

4

Bahá'u'lláh? Why were these writings so powerful? I wanted to know more.

Upon returning to Cape Cod, I contacted Ethelinda immediately and regularly attended firesides for approximately two years. Those two years were spent doubting, denying, and trying hard to refute everything I heard and all I read about Bahá'u'lláh and the Bahá'í Faith. But the answers were there. It could not be denied. It had to be true! And what beautiful people! All this time the Bahá'ís were so patient and so loving. They never became angry or annoyed by any question, reaction or response on my part.

In 1968, Martin Luther King was slain. All that I saw or heard through the news media during that week, made it very clear that the Bahá'í teachings and the World Order of Bahá'u'lláh were the only way to prevent such waste of human energy and life. What beautiful words such tragedies seem to inspire from our international leaders! It seemed these same words had been spoken a few years earlier when President John F. Kennedy was slain. Of what value are beautiful words without the hearts of men being changed? I found myself constantly repeating, 'Oh, if the world would just listen to Bahá'u'lláh and His Message, these things would not happen. If we followed in His Way, this would really be a better world.' So I became a Bahá'í.

In 1971, my Aunt Mae (who had also become a Bahá'í) and I were granted permission to go on pilgrimage to the Bahá'í World Center in Haifa, Israel. In the Archives Building on Mount Carmel, I saw for the first time the precious photograph of Bahá'u'lláh. I was devastated and completely overwhelmed! It was He whom I had seen in my bedroom fifteen years before — one year prior to hearing the word Bahá'í. Another long search had ended.

Winter Climb

by Larry Orloff

I was brought up in a culturally Jewish home, with the usual religious training culminating in a *bar mitzvah* at age thirteen. In February 1969, at age twenty-eight, I was working as a research scientist for a Massachusetts company in the Washington, DC, area, and had recently been transferred to the Boston area. Being a hiking enthusiast, I obtained the outings schedule of the Appalachian Mountain Club, and chose a moderate-level winter climb in the Mt. Lafayette area of the White Mountains.

This was my first trip to the White Mountains, and I decided to drive up at night in my Volkswagen bug, spend the night in a tent, and join the scheduled party in the morning. Being unfamiliar with the meeting location, I drove past it. It was after three a.m. before I finally found the place, and unsuccessfully attempted to sleep inside the car.

In the morning, when a group of hikers assembled near the car, I donned my snowshoes, hastening to join them. We ascended at what I thought was a rather fast pace for a moderate hike, and after some time I learned, to my surprise, that I had joined the wrong group. This was a relatively strenuous climb. The group I unwittingly joined was made up of AMC members who had planned the climb on an informal basis, while the officially scheduled party was to have met across the street from where I parked

We stopped before the final leg of the climb, which would be over snow-covered ice. I didn't have the crampon-like devices which, attached to the bottom of the snowshoes, would give them 'bite' into the ice, and by this time was feeling tired. I asked if I might wait there while the party climbed the peak, and descend with them when they returned. This suggestion was contrary to AMC rules against leaving individuals isolated on a mountain in winter, so one of the group graciously gave up his chance of completing a winter ascent of Mt. Lafayette, and volunteered to go down with me.

Reaching the parking area, I thanked him and prepared to drive home, when I discovered that my car was blocked by an auto belonging to another member of the party. To pass time until the others returned, my new-found companion and I went in his car to a nearby restaurant for coffee. He introduced himself as Sam McClellan, and in the course of our conversation, mentioned that he was a Bahá'í. My first reaction was that it must be some Japanese sect, but he told me more about it in a most comfortable, relaxed manner.

A few weeks later I wrote to a Bahá'í address listed in the Yellow Pages, and was sent literature and the name of a Bahá'í in a nearby town. At her fireside I asked about meetings in Cambridge, where I expected there would be a larger number of Bahá'ís, and was pleased to discover that meetings were held at Sam and Mimi McClellan's home. I became a regular seeker at their Friday night firesides, and enrolled in the Faith in May. The following April I married one of the fireside speakers.

A Spiritual Crown

by Sally Eiler

My roommate at college was very spiritual, and we were very close. One night she took me to a fireside. Up to that point, I hadn't the slightest idea that she was a Bahá'í or what the Bahá'í Faith was all about. Unfortunately, my first exposure to the Faith was extremely negative. The people leading the fireside were quite hostile and, it seemed to me, rather fanatical. They got into fierce arguments with almost everyone there, including the other Bahá'ís. I learned later that these same people were declared Covenant-breakers. At the time, I only knew that I didn't want to have anything to do with them or the Bahá'í Faith.

A year passed. Whenever someone mentioned the Bahá'í Faith, I immediately closed my mind and refused to discuss it, except to say that it seemed as narrow-minded as all the other religions. My poor, patient roommate continued to discuss the principles of the Faith without ever once mentioning their source. I agreed with everything she said, not realizing that I was privately supporting the very thing that I was so vehemently opposing in public.

One night I had a shattering dream, unlike any dream I have ever had. It was as clear and precise as watching a movie played out on a screen before my eyes. Throughout the dream I could simultaneously see myself asleep in bed, as a participant in the dream, and as a kind of super-ego suspended above my body, speaking directly to my soul.

As the dream began, I found myself coming out of a dark vortex surrounded by symbols of ancient religions and mystic philosophies. As the scene cleared, I was seated on a bus with a group of people who seemed to be fundamen-

8

talists of various types, religious and otherwise. They turned to me and told me emphatically that there was a man coming, and that I should not have anything to do with him, as he would be very bad for me. They began to argue amongst themselves about just who this man was. They were so busy arguing that when the man did come, they didn't see him. I was so upset by their bickering that I eagerly jumped off the bus to join him.

We began to run. At first the ground was rocky and difficult to travel, but as we struggled things began to get easier, the ground more rolling, the colors brighter. I looked to my left and saw a large red moon. I called the man's attention to the moon, but he told me to ignore it. I looked in front of me and saw a large yellow sun. We ran quickly toward it. As we approached, I saw other people, lined up two by two, walking toward it. Then we lifted off the ground and flew over the people's heads until we reached a large many-sided building that appeared as if it were made of carved ivory. Coming out of the doors were people of many religions. I remember greeting several, and saying 'Hare Krishna' to some Hindus.

We entered the building and found ourselves in a large circular room. A man in long white robes stood in the middle holding a crown. He was looking for a spiritual person on whom to place the crown. The priests were all acting very humble as if they thought they were unworthy. As soon as the man approached them with the crown, however, they would give away their desire by inclining their heads toward it. At that moment, the crown would quickly be drawn back.

While this was being repeated with all the priests, the man with me whispered, 'Sally, you are going to be a spiritual person.' I protested, and the man with the crown started to walk toward me. I tried to escape, and awoke in a

9

state of confusion, greatly perturbed by this dream. I immediately wrote it down.

I asked all my friends if they knew what the dream meant. Unfortunately, my Bahá'í friend had moved home and was unavailable to give me the answer that would have been so obvious.

At the time, I was studying eastern religions, especially Zen Buddhism. I continued with my studies, but something was just not right. I became more and more disillusioned with life, until I felt that there were no answers, that all existence was pointless.

Then my Bahá'í friend invited me to visit her for the weekend. I went in spite of (or perhaps because of) my poor spiritual state. She had made plans for the evening, and said that going out would make me feel better. While waiting for our ride, I turned to her with a sudden suspicion. 'Are we going to a fireside?' She rather sheepishly admitted that we were. At first I refused to go, but was so exhausted from my inner struggles that I had no fight left. So I agreed to go, but told myself that I just wouldn't listen.

When we arrived, the house was jammed with over twenty people. The host seemed nicer than the Bahá'ís I had met previously, but I was still on my guard. As we sat down, I resolved in my heart not to get involved in any arguments. If hostilities broke out, I would remain aloof. A young woman read a prayer with a great deal of feeling. I thought she sounded a bit melodramatic, but then she read the line, 'I will no longer be full of anxiety'. There I was, filled with anxiety, and suddenly a key turned in my heart. I began to listen.

Throughout the evening I found myself agreeing with everything that was said. My whole being seemed to be unfolding as I felt my tired, miserable self bathed in light and warmth. I realized that I was going to be a Bahá'í, in fact, already was one. It was all I could do to keep from laughing out loud at my previous stubbornness and sudden turnaround.

When the speakers had finished, I turned to my friend, took her hands, and said, 'Don't freak out, but I want to be a Bahá'í.' We both burst into tears and laughter, equally amazed at the mysterious ways of the Lord.

Lecture Series

by Ruth Alexander Foster

By February of 1939, I was at a dead end in my five-year search for a religion that would have a working solution for the world's problems and also offer personal consolation. One evening I went to an acquaintance's house to return Kahlil Gibran's *The Prophet*. I was quite intrigued with it and wished to discuss it with her, but as she was leaving for a lecture on comparative religions, I asked if I might accompany her. She said she would have to call as it was by invitation. I was invited.

The lecture was held in a little millinery shop on the ground floor of the Columbus, Ohio, YWCA. The room was done in blue, gray and rose, with mirror-backed shelves displaying colorful handmade hats. Little spindly-legged gold leaf chairs were scattered about the room. Very French. About a dozen people were there when we arrived. Behind a long table at the rear of the room stood a tall, striking woman of regal bearing — Olivia Kelsey. She had been a Shakespearean actress at one time, and had a dramatic, vibrant way of talking that held us all spellbound.

11

Olivia began with an explanation of the difference between religion and philosophy, and then discussed the Sabaean religion. In subsequent lectures she covered the lives and teachings of five prophets. The sixth lecture was on Muḥammad and Islám. When I realized she was putting Muḥammad on a par with Jesus, my heart began to pound and my throat became dry. I was outraged! Being from a Protestant background, I looked upon Muḥammad as an infidel, or worse. Only politeness kept me in my seat. I vowed never to return.

All the next week I argued with myself — to go, or not to go. Finally curiosity got the upper hand. I soothed my conscience with the thought that however wrong and misguided Olivia might be, she certainly seemed sincere. What's more, she fascinated me. She created an ambiance of expectation and hope, which buoyed us all up and made us look forward to the next meeting. We had some grand discussions.

The seventh lecture was about Persian history in the late seventeenth and early eighteenth centuries, including the Shaykhí movement. She ended the lecture by announcing that there would be an important message the following week and we would miss the chance of a lifetime if we did not hear it.

On that momentous evening I met the Báb. I say met, because Olivia made him so real, such a glorious and tragic Figure, that I believed I felt His presence in the room. She was so filled with love for the Báb that she transferred it to us. When I learned of His final days, I wanted to weep and my heart filled with anger toward His persecutors. It took me some time to get over the feeling that He was the most important Prophet.

The next few meetings were on Bahá'u'lláh (His station, lifelong martyrdom, excerpts from His Writings); 'Abdu'l-

Bahá (His appointment, station, long life of servitude and travel, excerpts from His Writings, His *Will and Testament*); and the Guardian, Shoghi Effendi, and his ongoing work of establishing the Administrative Order.

The last evening she invited us all to a study class, passed out literature, and urged us to obey the principle of independent investigation of truth by reading the Bahá'í Writings (there were not so many available then).

I felt it was all too good to be true, and that sooner or later in my reading, I would discover weaknesses. I did not. After much loving hospitality and infinite patience on the part of the Bahá'ís, I became a member of the Bahá'í Faith on November 19, 1939.

Once to Every Man and Nation

by K. Richard Tookey

For several years I lived within two blocks of the Peoria Bahá'í Center, and was not in the *slightest* curious about this strange-sounding group. Then I went to college in Greencastle, Indiana, at DePauw University, determined to become properly educated. Every week I stopped at the Greencastle Goodwill Store, looking for books to fill my empty bookcase. I bought many good books there, most of which to this day I have not read. One January day in my sophomore year, I bought two books on religion: *Buddhist Scriptures* (a Penguin Classic) and *The Bahá'í Faith: An Introduction* by Gloria Faizi. I put them away and would have forgotten them if the Bahá'í Faith hadn't been brought to my attention again within the week.

I was visiting one of my friends, a neighbor in the dorm, and it happened that the roommate of my friend's fiancée was there also. Somehow the topic of religion came up, and she mentioned in glowing terms the beliefs of a man who had given her a ride to Indianapolis. He was a Bahá'í. Now I admit that the beliefs of a man giving a ride to the roommate of the fiancée of a friend of mine is a rather tenuous connection to the Bahá'í Faith, but that reminder was just enough to get me to pick up my recently purchased book. I didn't put it down until I had read it clear through.

What that little book had to say impressed me thoroughly. Yet I saw no way to prove or disprove its claims. So I did what I had previously criticized many Christians for doing — I asked for a sign from God. 'If this is IT, God, let me know, will you?'

The next Sunday in church (I was a staunch Christian), it occurred to me during meditation that I ought to investigate this Bahá'í thing, and make a decision pro or con, instead of letting it float. Immediately the congregation stood up to sing a song I'd never heard before:

Once to every man and nation comes the moment to decide,
In the strife of truth with falsehood for the good or evil side
Some great cause, God's new Messiah, offering each the
    bloom or blight,
And the choice goes by forever twixt that darkness and that
    light.

Then to side with truth is noble when we share her wretched
    crust,
Ere her cause bring fame and fortune, and it's prosperous to be
    just
Then it is the brave man chooses while the coward stands aside,
'Til the multitude make virtue of the Faith they had denied.

By the light of burning martyrs Christ Thy bleeding feet we
  track,
Toiling up new Calvarys ever with the Cross that turns not
  back
New occasions teach new duties, time makes ancient good
  uncouth,
They must upward still and onward who would keep abreast of
  Truth.

Though the cause of evil prosper, yet 'tis Truth alone is strong,
Though her portion be the scaffold and upon the throne be
  wrong
Yet that scaffold sways the future, and behind the dim
  unknown,
Standeth God within the shadows, keeping watch above His
  own.
Amen.

I sank back into the pew, rather disturbed. A clearer
statement about making decisions about a new Messiah, I
could not have asked for. Yet I had almost talked myself
into dismissing it as mere coincidence when my eyes fell
upon the line 'James Russell Lowell — 1844'. That song
was written the very year the Bahá'í Era began!

On my way home from church, I stopped by the library
to look for Bahá'í books. On the way to the BP-360 shelf, I
passed by a poster which, in letters six inches high, pro-
claimed Bahá'u'lláh to the world. Why had I not noticed it
before?

After reading several books, I finally got up the nerve to
ask for Bahá'ís to contact me. A man named Bert called,
and offered to stop by. (It happens that Bert was the one
who had given a ride to the roommate of the fiancée of my
friend in the dorm.) At that time I was still a devoted member of the First Christian Church in Greencastle, and no
matter how many nice things Bahá'ís believed, Bahá'í still

15

sounded faintly like 'Moonie' to me. To my surprise, I found Bert was not only familiar with my denomination (the Disciples of Christ), but he had become a Bahá'í after attending Christian seminary! And to top it off, he was an alumnus of Eureka College, a Disciples of Christ school where my mother is a professor. His favorite professors were friends of mine! Images of 'Moonie' disappeared instantly. Who else but Bert could have been the first Bahá'í I met?

Later Bert took me to a community fireside, where I met several other Bahá'ís. I noticed a prayer book, opened it, and fell in love with the Short Obligatory Prayer. I bought a prayer book (the second Bahá'í book I owned) and began daily prayers the next day.

One week to the hour after my first fireside, I was walking around the campus with nothing to do, idly wondering if another fireside was scheduled. But I had forgotten the address and the phone number. At that moment a bicycle passed, and its rider fell not ten feet in front of me. I recognized Walt, a Bahá'í I had met the week before. He began to get back on his bike, with the air of one who has not been seen falling flat. With almost impish glee I destroyed his illusion by asking, 'Did you hurt yourself, Walt?' He walked his bike with me to my second fireside. I found out later that he had not fallen off his bike for three years, and to my knowledge, has not fallen off since.

Shortly afterwards, my inner resolve crystallized. I studied Bahá'í Writings all that summer, until seven months after that fateful visit to the Goodwill Store it was almost an afterthought to enroll. I later met the person who had donated Gloria Faizi's book to Goodwill. He told me it had gotten mixed in with his other books, and he had never intended to donate it. I offered to give it back, but he wanted me to keep it.

Of course all this could have been a series of coincidences, and I cannot prove it otherwise. But somehow, I think of it as more than that. For the rest of my life, God willing, whenever anyone sings '. . . and behind the dim unknown, standeth God within the shadows, keeping watch above His own', with tears in my eyes, I will answer, 'Amen'.

Second-Generation Bahá'í

by Claire Springston

My parents had the first Michigan wedding which was solely a Bahá'í service. Being born into a Bahá'í family, the most significant influences in my becoming a Bahá'í were my parents' love for the Faith and their obedience to the laws. They were dedicated to making the Faith a total way of life.

For instance, my whole family consulted about whether or not to homefront pioneer to Oak Park, Michigan. Pioneering meant that from the age of five, I was able to participate in the administrative activities of the Oak Park group — serving as an officer and choosing readings for the Feast when it was my turn.

Another way my parents instilled a love of the Cause was by telling stories of 'Abdu'l-Bahá. When I would come to my parents wanting to do certain things because 'everybody's doing it', these stories enabled me to accept the situation when I was told, 'You have a higher responsibility and what "everybody's doing" is not good enough.'

17

Some of my earliest memories include summers at Louhelen Bahá'í School. There I saw how people of various
racial and ethnic backgrounds loved each other and were
unified in the Faith. There were so few believers in the early
1950s, that those in the North Central States really felt like
one big family. Getting together at conferences and summer schools, we formed friendships which last even now –
linking pioneers throughout the entire world.

The conscious decision to become a Bahá'í started
forming at age twelve, when I went to a junior youth session
at Louhelen. Again I heard stories about 'Abdu'l-Bahá,
and after studying *Paris Talks,* it became the first Bahá'í
book I bought with my own money. I decided that I should
be able to answer questions people posed about the Faith,
rather than continuing to say, 'Ask my mother'. The teacher
I most remember from that summer was Lydmilla Van
Sombeck.

At next summer's junior youth session, I attended Helen
Reech's outstanding class on prayer. The first day's assign-
ment was to memorize the Tablet of Aḥmad. I gave up on
that task, but found that I learned it anyhow through osmosis, by hearing the others recite it. The most important
lesson from that class was that prayer, with faith, does
work.

This was dramatically proven to me when my family
wanted to go the the World Congress in London in April
1963. The Tablet of Aḥmad was recited a number of times
daily, and by January the family knew that the seemingly
insurmountable obstacles had been overcome.

As a thirteen-year-old at the World Congress, I found
that the diversity of the Faith was even greater than what I
experienced at Louhelen. Bahá'ís came from all over the
planet, wearing their native costumes and speaking their
own languages. There I *saw* that the Faith is truly a world-

18

wide religion, not just a concept in books. Until then I had seen only a few hundred Bahá'ís, but in London I saw thousands waiting to get into the Albert Hall. Standing in those lines, my teenage self became part of a giant, international family reunion of pioneers and of those who stayed to tend the home-front firesides.

All of these events were steps leading to a decision that really wasn't a decision. Raised in a Bahá'í home, and reinforced by Bahá'í summer schools and conferences, there was almost no question of whether or not to become a Bahá'í. What could possibly take its place? I had visited other churches, and thought them nice, but felt they lacked the substance and spiritual feeling of Bahá'í gatherings.

When I was fourteen, I read *Bahá'u'lláh and the New Era* on my own. That did it. Without a doubt, my belief was confirmed. Before that, I knew I was a Bahá'í, but this book told me *why.* Declaring was only a matter of form. I met with a nearby Assembly, answered a few questions, and was enrolled.

I feel that I did not really become a Bahá'í until college, however. I had just assumed that everyone had a unified family like mine. In college, I was surprised to meet people who hated their families and who disliked other kinds of people. That discovery made me want to share with others this Way of uniting the world.

College was a real period of search — not a time of doubt, but of reconfirmation. Prior to this time, I had read mainly the Writings of 'Abdu'l-Bahá. During my freshman year, I began studying Bahá'u'lláh's Writings for hours and hours, especially *Gleanings* and *The Kitáb-i-Íqán.* I decided then that I wanted to devote my entire life to the Cause of God. As an English major, I also came to a scholarly appreciation of Shoghi Effendi's use of the English language. From 'Abdu'l-Bahá's analogies one could get many, many meanings, but Shoghi Effendi was very specific, once one figured out what he meant. More and more these Writings confirmed my beliefs and my desire to share the Teachings with others.

As a second-generation Bahá'í, I wonder, had I not been raised in a Bahá'í family, would I have recognized the Truth for myself?

A Gift for Intercalary Days

by Betty Straubing

On a bulletin board in the laundromat of our little town in upstate New York, I noticed a small sign mentioning the Bahá'í Faith, with a phone number to call for information. My daughter said she had met some Bahá'ís in San Francisco and they were really nice people. There it dropped. I always wanted to check it out, but never got around to it.

Being a lunch lady in a primary school, amid the splatter of spilled milk and the clatter of silver, I hear a lot of stories from the children. One day, a kindergarten boy came to me, on fire with excitement, to tell me it was Intercalary Days in his religion. They give gifts and love one another.

Thank the good Lord that I took the time to ask, 'What religion?' 'Bahá'í!' he answered, and returned to his seat. I wrote a note — 'Am interested in Bahá'í. Call me.' — and sent it home in his lunch pail.

His mother called, answered my questions, and invited me to a fireside. That was it. After fifty years of searching, I had found my faith.

A Rebellious Youth

by Earl Ray Erickson

I first gained an interest in Seals and Crofts when I was fifteen years old, in the summer of '73. I was involved in cartooning as a hobby, with the goal of making it my career. That summer, after having created a new cartoon character, I saw Seals and Crofts on TV for the first time, and was surprised at how much Jim Seals looked like the character I had drawn up. That sparked my initial interest. I began listening more closely to their music, and soon became a devoted fan. At the time I was unaware that they were Bahá'ís.

I was a rebellious youth, and had many troubles at home. The following winter, things became nearly unbearable, so on Christmas Day I climbed out the window of our suburban home outside Salinas, California, and set off on my own.

I headed for Great Falls, Montana, the city where I was born. Most of my relatives lived there, and a cousin had said I was welcome to stay with him. So, with the reckless planning of the inexperienced, I bought a motorcycle with the money I'd saved while washing dishes for three months, and set off on a rainy day, with less than $35 to take me some 1400 miles into the Land of Winter. My cat, who I was packing on the back on the the motorcycle, ran away at the first rest stop. Once into the Sierra Nevada Mountains I hit a blizzard, and travel became very slow. When I reached Reno, Nevada, and walked into a Mc-Donald's restaurant, I noticed I had only $3 left. Eating was a luxury I'd have to do without for a while. After a day and a half in Reno, I managed to sell my bike for a loss of

21

$190. I got just enough for it to buy a bus ticket to Great Falls.

It was 20° below zero and snowing hard when I arrived. I walked about five miles before getting a ride to my cousin's house in Tracy, some fifteen miles outside Great Falls. He had just gotten married and was off on his honeymoon. When he got back, he realized that he didn't have room for me after all, so I went to stay with my grandparents. That was too much of an imposition on them, so an uncle in Tracy invited me to stay with him.

During this time, my older sister was busy trying to save my soul. She sent me literature on some sect of Christianity that she was currently involved in. My inner life was in a tumult after facing so many physical hardships, following a childhood full of comfort and security. I was searching deep for the meaning of life, and was desperately reaching out for God. I read all the literature that my sister sent, but many aspects of her beliefs were unsatisfactory to me. So much of it seemed to be just words, with the reality long forgotten.

I sincerely believed in God and wanted to obey Him. But I didn't know how. The frustration built until, in a prayer of sorts, I made a deal with God. I told Him that I wanted to live the right way, in accordance with His Will, but unless He would actually come down and tell me what His Will was, then I'd just have to do things my own way.

I really didn't believe that there was any way for God to come down and tell me what He wanted. I felt better after the prayer, though, because it gave me a direction to move in. I began building my own personal religion, deciding for myself what to believe and how to conduct my life.

Then one night shortly after my prayer, I was lying in bed listening to the radio, when I heard a short interview with Seals and Crofts, in which they played their song 'Hummingbird', and explained that it was about Bahá'u'lláh. That was the first I'd ever heard about the Bahá'í Faith. Because I was so attracted to Seals and Crofts, I was immediately touched and interested. I made a vow to check out the Bahá'í Faith someday, if I ever got the chance. I figured I'd have to travel to India or somewhere in the Middle East to learn about it, though.

The next day, I heard a radio advertisement explaining a little about the Faith and giving an address to write to for more information. After hearing it a couple of times, I finally found myself with a pen and paper, and managed to jot down the address. I wrote, and they sent me some introductory literature, prayers, and an invitation to attend a fireside. I started studying the literature and memorizing the prayers, but I couldn't attend a fireside because I lived so far from town, and had no transportation in the evenings.

During this time I went through a brief inner conflict. I realized that my personal religion was being built on shaky ground, because in reality I was very imperfect, and in no position to decide what was the truth. I needed an authority that I could trust, something outside myself. I thought about Bahá'u'lláh and wondered if maybe this was God's way of coming down and telling me what He wanted. In order to keep my side of the bargain, I felt it was my obligation to investigate further the Bahá'í Faith.

The obstacle to attending firesides was soon overcome when my uncle's wife decided that my hair was too long, so I'd have to cut it or leave. I chose to leave. My uncle planned to send me back to California, but I was determined to live or die in the wilderness before I would return home. Another uncle saved me from the dilemma when he invited me to stay with him in Great Falls. I was now close enough to walk to the firesides.

About a month after my sixteenth birthday, I attended my first Bahá'í meeting directly across the street from the hospital where I was born. I was overwhelmed by the spirit at that meeting. So many things that the Bahá'ís explained to me were things I'd thought about before, or were answers to questions I'd had. I knew right away that I had found what I was searching for. Still, I spent a month investigating deeper before I declared. I wanted to be sure that Bahá'u'lláh was truly a Messenger from God, and not just a wise and concerned individual trying to better the world. Once totally convinced, I joined the community of Bahá'u'lláh on May 9th, 1974. My parents became very friendly towards the Bahá'í Faith after they saw how it changed me, and they still encourage me in my efforts to serve it.

Black and White Together

by Betty J. Gilbert

I had never heard of the Bahá'í Faith until I came to South Carolina State College to work. There I met Dr Alberta Deas, a long-time member and staunch supporter of the Bahá'í Faith.

My new job brought me many problems, and with the problems came mental illness. 'D', as I fondly call her now, was cognizant of the troubles I was experiencing and helped by giving me a Bahá'í prayer book. She quoted passages from the Bahá'í scriptures relating to my tests and difficulties, and invited me to Bahá'í functions.

The first function I remember attending was a dinner

given in recognition of Human Rights Day. The Bahá'ís of Hilton Head had engaged 'D' to speak. We met at the Hilton Head Inn, where I encountered many delightful people. This was the first affair I can recall, with both whites and blacks present. 'D' 's talk was informative and interesting. The dinner was scrumptious. I thoroughly enjoyed it.

Later I heard that each meal had cost eight or ten dollars. I was astonished that 'D' had paid for me to attend. She never hinted about the cost. This impressed me. She later explained that Bahá'ís usually bear the expense when inviting non-Bahá'ís to their events.

That night, 'D', her two sons, and I stayed overnight with the hosts of the dinner affair. This was the first time I had stayed as the house guest of a white family. That weekend marked the beginning of my attendance at Bahá'í activities and of friendships with whites and other non-blacks.

One day, 'D' pointed out that I was an undeclared Bahá'í. Why didn't I take the next step by signing a declaration card? She had to explain about signing that card — signing anything frightens me. But I thought about joining a Faith that strives for world peace through unity of the races, and signed my declaration card in November 1978.

Every Friday Night

by Priscilla Jeanne Triplett

A little more than thirteen years ago I was a pre-school teacher at a community center on the far South Side of Chicago. During one of our many staff meetings a trip we had planned for the children was canceled, and the supervisor told us we would instead be visiting something called the Bahá'í House of Worship and afterwards would picnic at a nearby park.

The day of the trip I was still furious over the abrupt change in plans. It was raining. One of my two assistant teachers was absent. I had eighteen two-year-olds to escort to somebody's house of worship and then to a picnic. My sense of injustice was complete.

As our bus pulled up in front of a large, beautiful building, the rain stopped. As the children and I ascended the stairs, the sun came out and shone brightly. And as we neared the entrance, the children became very quiet. I looked at them and wondered what was happening. Never before had they behaved like this on a trip.

An elderly gentleman escorted our class to the front of the large auditorium, gave us a brief history of the Faith, and answered the children's questions. I was pleasantly surprised by the children's good behavior and by the fact that they remained quiet while in the auditorium which was for silent meditation.

As we left the building, I selected one of each of the pamphlets available at the door because I was genuinely attracted to this new religion and its teachings. However, it never dawned on me to look up the Bahá'í Faith in the Chicago telephone directory or to call the House of

26

Worship for more information. The pamphlets lay in my desk drawer for two years; every now and then I would read them and wonder.

Two and one half years later, having moved to Brooklyn, New York, I volunteered to teach a vacation Bible school for pre-schoolers at a Lutheran school where I normally taught fifth grade. The children in the Bible school class were to range from two to six years old.

The first day, a woman arrived with her son, age two years and three days. He was crying hard, mostly because he had never been away from his mother. I spoke lovingly but firmly to him: 'Joe (not his real name),' I said, 'You have one hour for crying and after that you must stop. Do you understand?'

'Yes,' he replied, sniffling.

At the end of an hour I said, 'Joe, your time is up. You must stop crying now.' To my surprise, he did exactly that!

At lunch, the seven other children said the traditional grace they had learned in their Lutheran homes while the new little boy, who was not from the Lutheran congregation, asked if he could say a prayer. When I said yes, he could, he closed his eyes and prayed. 'O God, guide me, protect me, illumine the lamp of my heart and make me a brilliant star. Thou art the Mighty and Powerful.'

I was most impressed! Imagine, a two-year-old child using words like 'protect' and 'illumine', 'brilliant', 'powerful' and 'mighty'!

Each day thereafter I shortened Joe's crying time by twenty minutes so that when I met him on Friday, and he was crying as usual when he arrived, I told him there was no more crying time. He stopped, said, 'Okay,' and was fine! I was shocked but tried not to show it.

One day the children were playing a game with my teenage assistant. One of them would call out his own

27

name, she would write it on the board, and the child would skip around the room saying, 'That's my name! That's my name!' Suddenly, my youngest student shouted, 'Write B—A—B on the board!'

The teenager looked at me, and when I nodded consent, she wrote 'Bab' on the blackboard. Joe smiled broadly and skipped around the room saying, 'That's the Báb! That's the Báb!'

Later, when Joe's mother came to pick him up, I told her what had happened, and she explained that Báb is a word that means 'gate'. Thus began my reintroduction to the Bahá'í Faith, in June of 1971.

Shortly thereafter, I attended a fireside hosted by Joe's parents in their Brooklyn home. Several Bahá'ís were present, in addition to quite a few folks who, like myself, had questions.

The fireside talk consisted of a brief history of the Faith covering the periods of the Báb, Bahá'u'lláh, and 'Abdu'l-Bahá. The basic principles of the Faith were enumerated: the fact that there is one God, the oneness of mankind, unity, elimination of extremes of wealth and poverty, establishment of a universal language, compulsory education, equality of men and women, establishment of a world government, independent investigation, and progressive revelation.

Coming from a Christian background, I was most impressed with the concept that the Spirit of Christ has returned in successive Manifestations and that each Prophet has taught different ways for man to relate to man, while never changing how man should relate to God.

After the presentation by the host, we all conversed in small groups while enjoying the refreshments. It was at this point that I brashly stated, 'If this is what a fireside normally covers, I don't need to attend any more of them!

28

I know all this. I want to know more! How do you learn more?'

A young Bahá'í lady named Jean, who had been silent most of the evening, spoke up. ' "To deepen in the Cause means to read the writings of Bahá'u'lláh and the Master so thoroughly as to be able to give it to others in its pure form . . ." ' She was quoting Shoghi Effendi. 'I host a deepening every Friday night at my house here in Brooklyn,' she continued. 'It's easy to get there by bus from where you live.' I had stated I was uncomfortable with New York City's subway system. 'You are welcome to come, bring your daughter Vicki, and spend the night if you like. I have an eleven-year-old sister, the same age as your daughter, and I'll invite her to come over on Saturday. The two girls can entertain each other.' I accepted, thinking how providential that I could pursue knowledge of this Faith while my daughter could perhaps meet a new friend her age.

One week later my daughter and I started on this adventure. The house was easy to locate and we were greeted at the door by Jean's grandmother who was so gracious, pleasant and hospitable that I was a little surprised to learn later that she was not a Bahá'í.

We were a little early since I had allotted extra time in case we got lost. While we waited for others to arrive, Jean and I became acquainted by telling each other a little about ourselves. It was a pleasant situation and I found myself very relaxed, which was a bit unusual for me. I noted Vicki was relaxed also. I had made a practice of looking for cues about new personalities by observing children's reactions. I felt they had an innate sense of character.

As each of the others arrived for the deepening, we were introduced. Jean's grandmother invited Vicki to join her upstairs where they could watch television. At the designated time we were all seated comfortably in the living room and each person took a turn reading a prayer. Jean allowed me to use her prayer book so that I could participate.

The prayers fascinated me. They seemed to have so much depth and insight into my personal needs. I was also struck by the diversity of races, education and backgrounds exemplified by this group of people. There were blacks, whites, former Christians, Jews and Muslims of various ages with ethnic accents, all reading prayers with great reverence and love.

Using a study guide compiled for youth, we took turns reading aloud selected quotations from the Writings of Bahá'u'lláh and 'Abdu'l-Bahá. Then we each in turn responded to the discussion topics suggested at the end of the readings. It did not seem to matter to the others, who were all Bahá'ís, that I was not, and my opinion seemed just as valid to them as did their own. There was no air of condescension or argument or politely stifled intolerance. I was perfectly at ease and barely conscious of the fact that my daughter and I were there for the first time. Since I was normally very self-conscious and not too trusting, it was most unusual for me to be so at ease with people whom I had only met that evening, and extremely unlike me to spend the night at the home of anyone other than my own family members.

We concluded the deepening with another round of prayers, and conversed while enjoying the refreshments Jean had prepared. After the others left, Jean and I continued talking until almost midnight. She suggested we read prayers again before retiring, and quoted a passage about the importance of reading from the Writings morning and night. My daughter came downstairs to sleep with me on a very comfortable pull-out sofa. There was such peace. We rested well.

The following morning, Jean insisted she must fix breakfast for us and smilingly dismissed all of my efforts to assist. She stated that she wanted to serve us and proceeded to do so. We met her younger sister, who also lived in the house, and later we met her mother and her youngest sister who became Vicki's immediate friend and companion. The girls went out with Jean's mother so we had the day to shop, take care of Jean's chores, and to chat. We talked about a number of things: jobs, schools, children, men, marriage, divorce, and always I asked, 'What's the Bahá'í concept?' and always Jean patiently answered.

I was impressed with the combination of qualities she displayed: strength yet humility, energy yet calm, no unnecessary chattering, a definite wisdom of speech about things that were important to me. She quoted Bahá'u'lláh, 'Abdu'l-Bahá, Shoghi Effendi, or the Universal House of Justice, and answered my questions about their spiritual stations, Bahá'í administration, the Covenant, and local Assemblies. My questions were unceasing. I felt surely I must be a bother, but she never exhibited any impatience. When I inquired about her use of verbatim statements from the Writings, she quoted Shoghi Effendi about giving the Message in its pure form.

Because my questions were still flowing and I was so at peace, I accepted Jean's invitation to spend another night. Vicki and I left reluctantly on Sunday afternoon after promising Jean we would return the following weekend. Jean's youngest sister would also stay over and she and Vicki had made plans to go roller-skating.

Every Friday evening thereafter, my daughter and I went to Jean's home. I attended the deepenings, we spent the weekend, and we both enjoyed ourselves. I learned about the Faith, and Vicki learned about the Faith and Brooklyn. We had both formed wonderful friendships.

31

I was in awe of the things I was learning about the Bahá'í Faith. Yet I felt I could not become a Bahá'í because I could never live up to the standards. I knew there was no clergy and that each Bahá'í should teach. I felt I would never know enough to teach the Faith or have the inner strength to live the life.

Through the weeks I acquired a prayer book and *Bahá'í World Faith*, both gifts from Jean, and when I was at home I would read, read, read! The Writings entranced me by their beauty; they made me think, analyze, weigh, and meditate. Sometimes I would read a passage, stop, walk away from the book, think about what I'd read, then go back, pick up the book, and read some more. I also observed and enjoyed the loving family-like relationships among the Bahá'ís. The genuine caring, courtesy, and warmth each person displayed towards the others, as well as to me and mine, made deep impressions.

During this period I voluntarily attended church services only when I was asked to sing. (I had been singing in churches since I was four years old and had always felt my ability to sing was a gift from God that must be shared with others in praise of Him.) When I read that Bahá'u'lláh had written, 'Intone, O My servant, the verses of God ...', I started singing the Bahá'í prayers when I was alone.

I was required to attend Friday morning worship services with my fifth grade class, but could not bring myself to kneel or to take communion. Although I believed in God and Christ, I had rejected the genuflecting and mass confessions. It was causing the church pastors some consternation, but I explained that I could not submit to guidelines for worship which I felt man had established, and which varied from church to church even within the same denomination.

The first Friday in October of 1971, Vicki and I went to

Jean's house as we had been doing regularly for four months. The deepening went as usual with a round of prayers, topic readings and discussion, and concluded with another round of prayers. (There were a few more Bahá'ís than usual in attendance and each one read a prayer.) The person seated to my right read aloud first and the readers proceeded counterclockwise to the Bahá'í on my left. He read a prayer for spiritual qualities, number sixty-eight in the green prayer book. Then he handed his book to me. Since I didn't want to shuffle through the book looking for a short prayer, as I was inclined to do, I started reading where the book was already opened. It was prayer number sixty-nine. I read aloud:

He is the Gracious, the All-Bountiful!

O God, my God! Thy call hath attracted me, and the voice of Thy Pen of Glory awakened me. The stream of Thy holy utterance hath enraptured me, and the wine of Thine inspiration entranced me. Thou seest me, O Lord, detached from all things but Thee, clinging to the cord of Thy bounty and craving the wonders of Thy grace. I ask Thee, by the eternal billows of Thy loving-kindness and the shining lights of Thy tender care and favor, to grant that which shall draw me nigh unto Thee and make me rich in Thy wealth. My tongue, my pen, my whole being, testify to Thy power, Thy might, Thy grace and Thy bounty, that Thou art God and there is none other God but Thee, the Powerful, the Mighty.

I bear witness at this moment, O my God, to my helplessness and Thy sovereignty, my feebleness and Thy power. I know not that which profiteth me or harmeth me; Thou art, verily, the All-Knowing, the All-Wise. Do Thou decree for me, O Lord, my God, and my Master, that which will make me feel content with Thine eternal decree and will prosper me in every world of Thine. Thou art in truth the Gracious, the Bountiful.

Lord! Turn me not away from the ocean of Thy wealth and the heaven of Thy mercy, and ordain for me the good of this world and hereafter. Verily, Thou art the Lord of the mercy-seat, enthroned in the highest; there is none other God but Thee, the One, the All-Knowing, the All-Wise.

'Abdu'l-Bahá

After a few moments of reverent silence, the other guests started moving toward the refreshments. My eyes were closed and I remained still as it dawned on me the prayer I had just read was from my heart! It was as if it had been written to express everything I believed and felt! My soul was on fire with love!

When I opened my eyes there was no one seated in the living room but me. Jean was closing venetian blinds at the windows. I said, 'Jean, what do you say when you want to become a Bahá'í?'

In her usual patient manner of responding to my never-ceasing questions, she said, 'You tell a Bahá'í.'

'Jean,' I said slowly, 'I want to be a Bahá'í!'

'Yá Bahá'u'l-Abhá!' she shouted. Everyone came running back into the room. 'She's a Bahá'í! She just declared!' Hugs! Kisses! Joy!

Guaymi Dawn Song

by Vinson Brown

While being trained as a scientist in anthropology and biology at the University of California at Berkeley, I gradually lost my belief in religion because it seemed so dogmatic and narrow-minded, and I became an atheist. Then in 1935, in the jungles of Panama and Costa Rica, I was collecting specimens for museums and happened to obtain as an assistant a Guaymi Indian youth, Chio Jari. He came from the wild mountains of the Serrania de Tabasara, where his tribe was still independent of the white people. We worked together for one year and I was astonished by his wonderful nature, his cooperation, trustworthiness, courage, humbleness, purity, and beautiful spirit.

Early one morning, I chanced to see him standing on a rock below a beautiful waterfall in the mountains, singing his dawn song. It wasn't just a song, but a tremendous prayer, so filled with Spirit, pouring out of him towards the sky, that I was literally able to feel it like a living thing. This completely changed my attitude and when I returned to the United States, I began to study all the religions of the world with an open mind. I recognized in all of them the same beautiful teachings and realized their essential unity.

Just before entering the army in 1944, while working in the Office of War Information in San Francisco, a lady there asked me why I was reading a book on Buddhism. When I explained my search for the meaning of religion, she gave me a copy of *Bahá'u'lláh and the New Era*. This led me to take a course on the Bahá'í Faith taught by Marion Holley. All my questions were intelligently answered, and I became a Bahá'í.

Years later, the Spirit which Chio Jari gave to me in 1935 came full circle back to the Guaymi Indians through my son. An ancient prophecy of the famous Guaymi holy man, the Ngobo Ulikron, told the tribe that one day they would fall into a time of darkness of the Spirit, but that a noble blind man would lead them out of this darkness into the light. By the time my son Kirby pioneered to Panama in 1959, the lowland Guaymi were in a bad way, and even the mountain Guaymi were being corrupted by white civilization. However, there was a blind man among them who was noted for his wisdom and purity. Kirby found this blind man and in four days of discussion, the man was convinced that the Bahá'í Faith was the dawn of a New Day. He became a great Bahá'í teacher, and now there are thousands of Guaymi who are Bahá'ís.

Hidden Treasure

by Terralin Carroll

I was just a child of six when I dreamt of the old man in the rose garden. He wore Arabian clothing, a white turban and long flowing robes of white and brown. A snow-white beard framed his kindly face. He beckoned to me. I felt a little shy at first, but his smile reassured me. He seemed to say, 'Come, see, I know a wonderful secret.' I put my small hand in his and we walked among the flowers.

He told me many strange tales, of valleys shrouded in mists, and great treasures hidden from the eyes of men, and of a wondrous Prince. It was said of this Prince that He was a great Prince, but that the people did not know this. They would not understand until the Kingdom had been restored.

The years went by and life held many challenges. In time I forgot about the old man in the garden and his stories.

I started college, majoring in history, and began to think about the growth and development of man in new ways. I had been naive in many of my perceptions of the world. There was so much I had simply taken for granted. I began to re-examine the tenets of my faith, especially those things I had been told concerning the Second Coming of Christ.

I came across a book written by a young Iranian girl who was a devout Muslim. She had been educated in the West and was concerned about the backwardness of her people. She traveled from village to village, teaching the people what she could about simple health practices. Included in the book were beautiful poems she had written of her love for God and her fellow man.

I thought to myself, 'This woman is a much better Christian than I have ever been. If Christ returned in the way I have been taught to believe, what of those good people of other faiths, such as this Muslim woman?'

I was certain the Second Coming had to be for all people of all faiths. And yet, how could this be? Would a devout Jew or Buddhist be able to identify and respond to the return of Christ? I knew God's love was for everyone. If there was a Second Coming it would have to be in such a way that would give each person on earth an equal chance. It could not be for Christians only. I began to pray for understanding of this problem. There had to be an answer.

One night after meditating on this question I had a puzzling dream. I was in a valley with a large group of people. We wandered aimlessly about, waiting for something. Then I saw a Man come down from the mountains.

37

He had a beard and shoulder-length hair. He wore long flowing robes and sandals on His feet. With a shock, I realized the Man was Christ.

I expected people to gather palm branches and lay them at His feet, to sing hosannahs in praise of Him, but to my surprise, they did nothing. He walked among the people, who seemed not to notice Him. He stopped and looked directly into peoples' faces, but they turned away as if embarrassed.

When I awoke from the dream I felt certain there was some hidden meaning there, but I could not imagine what it was. Christ had walked among the people and yet they had not acknowledged Him. Why? I continued to pray for understanding. Again I had an unusual dream.

In this dream I felt oppressed by the crowded city. I walked for blocks until I came to an open meadow. There was the barest hint of dawn on the horizon. I sat down on the grass and picked one of the beautiful wild flowers. As I examined the flower, I felt a presence, like a stirring of wind in the tall grass.

I looked up and saw a man coming across the meadow. He walked with such dignity and grace that I knew he was a man of God. He wore a white turban and long robes of black and white. A snow-white beard framed his face. His eyes were crystal blue like an early morning sky.

He stood before me and I asked him a question. 'Why isn't man as beautiful as the flowers?' He looked away for a moment and I saw a sadness in his eyes that told me he had seen men do worse things than I could ever imagine. Then he looked at me and said, 'Because a man does not live in the Will of God as much as a flower does.'

Then he spoke to me without words. He told me of the flowers and how each one has its own special beauty. The flowers do not envy one another, nor feel that any one flower is in some way better than another. He smiled as if to say, 'Take heart. There is a great secret yet to be discovered.'He looked towards the East and the rising sun. I followed his gaze. The sun appeared upon the horizon streaming vibrant rays of golden light. It seemed as if all creation, even every small blade of grass, rejoiced in the warmth of the morning sun.

When I awoke I found myself sitting up in bed. I could still feel the joyousness of the sun shimmering all about me. I knew this had been no ordinary dream. I decided that the venerable man of God must have been an ancient prophet. Perhaps from his writings I would find the answers I was seeking.

I read all through the Old Testament, hoping to find something he had written. But nowhere could I find anything with his wise and gentle spirit upon it. Greatly disappointed, I decided to try the library. I had no idea what to look for. I walked down the rows of books hoping that by chance I might find what I was seeking. But I found nothing.

Seven years passed and there was still nothing to lead me to the wise man of God. Perhaps it had, after all, been only a dream. Then through the World Future Society I became acquainted with an organization called People for Peace. They were just beginning publication of a new magazine, *Peace Digest.* I was happy to work with them on their magazine. To promote *Peace Digest,* I attended a Peace Fair.

One of the booths at the Fair caught my attention. It had in bold letters: 'BAHÁ'Í FAITH — SETTING THE STAGE FOR WORLD UNITY!' I had never heard of the Bahá'í Faith and had no idea what it could be, but I decided to find out. There was no one at the booth, but several pamphlets were set out with the invitation to take one. One of the pamphlets caught my eye. On it was a drawing of an elderly bearded man. A white turban crowned his head. I stared at it in amazement. Could this be the man whom I had been seeking for so long? The pamphlet said his name was 'Abdu'l-Bahá and he had been born in the year 1844. It had never occurred to me to look for a man who lived in this century. I had assumed the man of God of my dream was a prophet from Old Testament times.

A few days later I got enough courage to call the Bahá'í phone number. My husband was a strict Mormon and I knew he would not approve of my investigating this new Faith. I was surprised at the friendliness of the Bahá'í who answered the phone. I explained I had no transportation. That was all right. He was happy to come to get me.

During the drive to the Bahá'í home I thought again of 'Abdu'l-Bahá. The pamphlet said he was from Iran. The man in my dream had beautiful blue eyes. I thought this would be unusual for an Iranian, but the features were exactly as I recalled them. Could it be the same man?

As I walked into the Bahá'í home, the first thing that caught my eye was a portrait of 'Abdu'l-Bahá. The artist had portrayed him with such vibrancy and sensitivity that he seemed to be smiling in welcome. His eyes were a clear blue.

As the evening progressed I became more and more astonished at all Mr and Mrs Stephens told me of the Báb, Bahá'u'lláh and 'Abdu'l-Bahá. It was the story of Christ all over again. Finally Mrs Stephens said, 'We believe Bahá'u'lláh is Christ come again.' It was a momentous statement. The Second Coming had taken place as it had before, in a backward part of the world, amid great struggle and sacrifice. The Messiah had walked among the people and they had not acknowledged Him.

As the fireside came to a close, I decided to tell Mr and Mrs Stephens about my dream of 'Abdu'l-Bahá. I told them how he had spoken of the flowers and that I had searched for him for many years.

They came and put their arms around me and all three of us began to cry. Just at that moment their son came down the stairs. He didn't know why we were crying, but it made him cry too. Soon our tears turned to laughter.

Mr Stephens showed me some photographs of 'Abdu'l-Bahá. One of them was taken in 1912 when he was in Chicago. In this picture he was slender and wore a long black robe exactly like the wise man I had dreamed about. The second picture had been taken some years later just before his death. In this photograph he wore a lighter colored robe and he appeared a little heavier.

With a shock, I remembered when years before as a child I dreamed of the kindly old man in the rose garden. He had told me of valleys shrouded in mist and great treasures hidden from the eyes of men. I had found the treasure at last.

Fanatical Search

by Vito Benenati

After four years in the Air Force I was released from active duty, having experienced the insanity of Viet Nam. The spectacle from which I had just returned seemed quite unreal, but to my horror, the situation I found back home in Woodmere, New York, was just as strange. The radio was constantly warning of the dangers of heroin and giving guidance as to where to get help. A number of people I had

41

known were no longer with us, either because they had lost their lives in the war or through the misuse of drugs at home. I looked to the older people and beheld only daily routines, fatigue, stress, material existence and unhappiness. Everyone seemed to be caught in a trap of one type or another.

One day in the spring of 1971, as I crossed the street by the house in which I had grown up, I became definitely aware that there was an answer. At that moment I was touched, and the call to search became conscious within me.

My search took me through many different schools of thought, including philosophy, yoga, meditation and parapsychology. From each I acquired different pieces of information, and began building a framework of what I thought life to be. At all times, I was definitely aware of trying to tear away a veil from above my head.

As the next few years unfolded, the intensity of my search increased to fanaticism. I ran to everyone I heard of who might know the answer. I was meditating so much that I found myself living in a vacuum, totally abstract, not being able to relate to anything around me. I kept a diary, placing these abstract thoughts on paper. This was the only means by which my thoughts found expression in the physical world.

One night while driving home, I screamed out, 'What is driving me!?' I confronted the possibility of giving up and my reponse was an emphatic, 'No!' I knew I couldn't stop, no matter what happened.

One evening shortly after that, while sitting alone in the living room, reading what I had written in my diary over the years, a familiar thought from Jesus came to mind: 'Ye will know the tree by its fruit.' As I read, I became aware that this tree I was examining was quite barren. Upon reading the last sentence, I wrote in large letters across the page, 'The end, new perspective, new approach.' Suddenly my mind was crystal clear. I had emptied myself. I didn't know what the truth was, but I knew I didn't have it.

As I sat back in the chair, I became aware of a gentle illumination that filled the room but didn't appear to come from any particular point. Just then, the words came very clearly to my mind: 'You're looking for God.' Then the light faded. This was quite a revelation to me because I really didn't know that that's what I was doing. Not knowing whether I was speaking out loud or thinking, I acknowledged the fact that yes, indeed, I was looking for God.

But how was I supposed to find Him? The different philosophies I was in touch with were all saying, 'This way!' 'No, this way!' At that moment, the wonderful light returned, filling the room (I feel so warm recalling the experience), and I realized that if the knowledge of God were available, there must be a point from which that knowledge comes. There must be a Source. The light faded and my whole being filled with anticipation, for I knew I was about to find that Source.

For the next two days I was really able to listen to people when they spoke, because I wasn't getting any interference from my own static. On the evening of the second day, in a gathering of some friends from my parapsychology organization, Ray Lewis began speaking about Bahá'í. He wasn't being permitted to speak freely, so I found myself defending him. I wasn't able to learn much about the Faith that night, but I pleaded with Ray to get me some books.

A few days later, Gloria Faizi's *The Bahá'í Faith: An Introduction* was in my possession. I opened the book and began to read with a thrill of expectation I could hardly contain. I laid my eyes on the words of Bahá'u'lláh for the first time. I didn't know who Bahá'u'lláh was and I couldn't say His name properly, but the Voice I heard when I read those words was the same Voice I had heard in the Ten Commandments as a child, One I seemed to have forgotten. I had found the Source of the knowledge of God, and His Voice was loud and clear.

Soon afterwards, I attended my first fireside. My deepest impression of the people I met was that they all seemed so real. I declared my belief in Bahá'u'lláh that night, and upon doing so, had the clear experience of feeling my feet touch the ground. I had journeyed into outer space in search of my Beloved and found Him here, on Long Island.

Let Your Fingers
Do the Walking

by Jill Johnston

We found the Bahá'í Faith by letting our fingers do the walking through the Yellow Pages. We were really 'shopping' for a religious affiliation. Having been raised a Methodist, and having attended other Christian churches, I knew they didn't hold the fulfillment we sought, so I didn't call any of the mainline denominations. There were only three other churches listed within reasonable travel distance.

Mormon: At that time there was racial discrimination practiced in the Church hierarchy, so I didn't contact them. My God didn't care about skin color as a basis of qualification.

44

Seventh-Day Adventist: I knew little about the Adventists, so I called, and the pastor came to our home to help us in our study. After a few weeks we recognized that literality confines and limits God and our own understanding as well. It also demands belief in what seem to be some very unlikely occurrences.

Finally I called the Bahá'í Faith. I thought it was a Jewish group. My initial two-hour conversation was with Connie Stride. I taped my questions and her responses to share with my husband Gary who works nights. I was flabbergasted and elated! *My* ideas were so unorthodox compared to the doctrines of churches I was acquainted with, that I expected to find something Gary could be happy with, while the church and I could get by with an attitude of mutual toleration. But here was an organized religion that wasn't afraid of questions, that knew the reality of one Source, and that had common-sense teachings and explanations! I fired question after eager question, and back came sensible, fulfilling answers. No hocus-pocus! I made a date to attend a fireside.

Gary was initially skeptical of that foreign-sounding name (there are so many new cults nowadays), but as he listened to the enthusiastic explanations to each of my queries, he became increasingly impressed. Our first contact was in January 1977, and by April (Jamál 134 Bahá'í Era) we had declared our belief in the Faith of Bahá'u'lláh.

Thrill of Recognition

by Violet Dutov Tichenor

I was born in 1925 in Saskatchewan, Canada, in the village of Veregin, one of the three original settlements formed by the Doukhobors when they came from Russia in the late 1890s. By my time, the group had split. The more zealous had moved on to British Columbia. The ones who remained (my parents among them) were disillusioned with religion because of the graft and immorality of their leaders. They were weak in observing their religious and moral teachings, but were kept out of the mainstream of Canadian life by the differences in language, dress and customs. From earliest childhood, I was strongly aware of this disintegration of moral life in the community. My childhood play revolved around the fantasy of living in a world with people who were vital, honest and loving.

When I was sixteen, I left the Doukhobor community and found work in the city of Winnipeg. I expected to find the qualities I was looking for in this 'Canadian' society, but soon found that they weren't there either. I attended various churches from time to time, but what was said there seemed to have no bearing on life. I did not think I was looking for God. I had received so little religious training that I didn't think in those terms. I was merely looking for human truth and goodness.

When I was twenty, I became acquainted with Ola Pavlowska. Ola was not a Bahá'í then, but she thought I would be interested in meeting some people she knew, and took me to what I eventually learned were Bahá'í firesides. The Bahá'ís of Winnipeg were doing indirect teaching in those days, stressing only the social principles. They never mentioned the Faith or any of its Central Figures, for fear of frightening off their contacts with the strange names. I enjoyed the meetings and relaxed in the congenial atmosphere.

One afternoon over tea, one of the young girls self-consciously dropped the word 'Bahá'í' in conversation. I felt a deep thrill of recognition and the word echoed and re-echoed down the corridors of my soul. I wondered at this but said nothing to anyone. For eight months I attended firesides and read a book or two, but did not understand that I needed to accept or reject anything.

Then one Sunday I awoke feeling very loggy and dull. That afternoon I attended the fireside, still feeling drowsy and unfocused. While listening to the speaker, I suddenly heard my own inner voice, in a tone of wonder and exultation, saying, 'I am a Bahá'í!' At that moment, all my senses expanded and sharpened to an almost unbearable degree. I felt as though I entered into all the people in the room and was aware how each of them was feeling. Even the pattern of the chintz covers on the furniture came alive; a dynamic interplay between the shapes and colors made the pattern in the fabric seem to flow. I felt myself in the large maple trees outside the window. It was late fall and the trees were dormant, but I felt the stilled life and the patience within them. This heightened state seemed to last for many minutes, but when I came to, I found that I had not missed a word of the talk.

Stunned and shaken, I waited until the meeting was over and the non-Bahá'ís had gone home. Then I told the Bahá'ís of my experience. They arranged for me to meet with the Local Spiritual Assembly to be officially enrolled in the Faith. I never felt that I 'became' a Bahá'í. I was always a Bahá'í and just took some time to mature to an awareness of the fact.

Prison of Self

by John Jacob Phillips

I might easily have found the Bahá'í Faith at my doorstep. At one time, a fellow student told me about the Central Figures of the Faith, but I was so involved with academic study that I paid no mind. Two neighbors in adjacent houses were active Bahá'ís, but I was concerned with other matters. As it turned out, it was necessary to go far away from home before I could recognize and enter my true home — the Bahá'í Faith.

I was raised in the Jewish tradition. My grandfather Jacob had helped found a small synagogue in Lynn, Massachusetts, my home town. I was confirmed at a *bar mitzvah* ceremony in that synagogue at age thirteen. While attending public school in Lynn, I also studied at the I. L. Peretz Yiddish School, and in this way gained a sense of Jewish history and culture. I thought of myself as a Jew in every sense of the word, and took pride in the values and achievements of the Jewish people. The emphasis placed on truth, justice, and obedience to law greatly influenced my development.

While a student at the Massachusetts Institute of Technology, periods of intense academic concentration alternated with intervals of search for personal identity. During such times, Christianity (whose claims I had never considered seriously) challenged my thinking, and seemed to hold vital clues about my own purpose in life, although I could not reconcile this with my Jewish background. In time, the struggle for identity became a serious obstacle to progress in my studies, and was an important factor in my decision to withdraw from school.

After a sojourn in the business world, I resumed my studies, but in a liberal arts curriculum more suited to my pressing questions. Enrolling at Boston University in the Department of Philosophy in 1963, I hoped to find a training ground where I could develop methods for exploring claims to truth. I became familiar with the perpetual attempts of great thinkers to unravel the 'mystery of existence', and acquainted myself with many of the historical world religions. At this point, I was very skeptical and tended to regard the followers of organized religious systems as those who exemplified what Socrates referred to as 'the unexamined life'. I had already disassociated myself from Judaic practice (although retaining respect for its values), and found that the various schools of academic philosophy were unable to fulfill my craving for meaning in life. Faced with a void, I drifted toward an existentialist view of the world, but concluded that existentialism was barren of purposefulness. Finally, abandoning the world of ideas, I sought meaning in action.

The war in Viet Nam provided an opportunity to become committed to a moral cause. Guided by my own conscience, and subject to the influences of conflicting social forces, I pieced together a loose fabric of moral principles. I knew these were based on premises that were at best inconsistent and partial understandings, without more than a subjective standard of truth, but I acted upon them in order to propel myself out of contemplation and into action. These principles would be tested in the process — with myself as the guinea pig. I joined others who shared some of these principles and began to call myself a pacifist.

To carry the moral equation that 'war is evil' to its logical conclusion became my goal. Initial protest letters to editors and elected representatives soon gave way to rallies

49

and picketing against the war effort. Personal skills in writing and speaking were stimulated through these activities, and this became a motivating factor in itself as I gained recognition from those with whom I worked.

Soon, however, the path became less clear. The question of confrontation entered. My impulse was to back up my principles with readiness (and later, eagerness) to take risks for what I espoused. Civil disobedience (a contradiction in terms, as it became apparent afterward) was a new dimension of involvement against the forces that I thought were responsible for war. Protest became rebellion against established authority, and with it, a Pandora's box of complications was unloosed. The question became: How far should I go? There seemed no clear answer, so I kept setting my own limits, then passing them. To sound the depths of my commitment, I assumed I had to increase the level of risk.

In a short time I was dangerously isolated, but this was the price of my quest. My actions had entered an area where they were clearly provocative and illegal. Resistance to the military draft resulted in a felony conviction, and I spent a year and a half in a federal prison. There, my attitude only hardened, and the difficulties of confinement became a self-confirmation. To remain consistent, I continued protesting even in prison, and upon release I broadened my protest to include criticism of the penal system itself. This was done with the conviction that I was serving the cause of truth.

Since I had not 'learned my lesson' from the time in prison, it was inevitable that I would be returning. I resumed provocative activity. In May of 1969, I allied myself with a group of others to destroy Selective Service records in Chicago. We had not planned to escape, but rather to court arrest as a means of forcing the public to respond to what we had done. We were caught in the act, as expected, but I experienced the shock of realizing that I had gone too far. This insight eventually led me to question the basis of earlier actions and to realize how far I had strayed from the path of truth.

In the months between arrest and the scheduled federal trial, while free on bail, the full impact of that recognition hit me. A veil had been torn away and it left me reeling, unable to cope with the realization that I had erred so grievously, beginning with the decision to involve myself in political affairs. I sought refuge in solitude. What was at first merely a retreat to rethink became another calculated risk, for I had become a fugitive from justice. For a year and a half, I secreted my whereabouts from family and friends, adopted a new name, and tried to piece together a credible and viable personal role. I knew it could not last. I could not continue to relate to others on the basis of deception. I had betrayed truth, but could not accept life without it.

In desperation, I risked a note to a friend, who I knew had become a Bahá'í after a long and difficult struggle in her own life. I hoped her response would contain some clue to help me extricate myself from this labyrinth of hopelessness. She invited me to visit and I went at once — daringly hitchhiking 1,000 miles to reach her. She was host to a number of Bahá'ís who had gathered from various places for a teaching activity designed to reach the Spanish-speaking population. Without hesitation, I fell in among the friends and found that their fellowship and unity made me happy. I felt a part of the group, and after a few days in their company I wanted to remain with these souls.

While a guest of some of the believers at a nearby Indian reservation, I spent an agonizing, sleepless night wrestling inwardly with the seeming impossibility of my situation,

51

for I was not free to become a Bahá'í. Like my namesake, Jacob of the Old Testament, who wrestled with an angel and at dawn received his new identity as Israel, I found relief at last. I decided to accept Bahá'u'lláh, and prayed that He would help me to do whatever was necessary to transform my life into one of service for His Cause.

Before anyone else in the house awoke, I arose and signed a card declaring my faith in Bahá'u'lláh and accepting His laws. I signed my true name, after having concealed it for so long. Then I stood at the window, facing eastward as the sun rose, and was filled with a radiant joy that I had never known before. It was like the embrace of an angel, and it gave me hope that even the most tangled circumstances could be overcome by the love of God.

Shortly after my declaration of faith, I formed a plan to surrender to the federal authorities and accept the consequences of my offenses. Because the crime had taken place in Chicago, I directed myself to that city. When I learned that the National Bahá'í Convention was to be held near Chicago in a few days, I wondered if it would be possible to attend. The answer came swiftly into my heart: I could reach Wilmette by Friday evening, attend the Convention on Saturday and Sunday, then proceed early Monday to surrender at the Federal Building in Chicago.

Everything went smoothly. My identity was protected while the Convention was in progress, as I absorbed as much as I could of what it is to be a Bahá'í. A Bahá'í from Chicago, who had afforded me hospitality during my stay, drove me to the Federal Building but could not bear to accompany me closer than a block away. Later, he and others visited me at the Cook County Jail, where I awaited sentencing. The sentence was merciful — three years of incarceration, of which I served two before my release on parole to Boston, Massachusetts. Those years became a time of preparation, of growing and deepening in the Faith I had embraced (and been embraced by), learning prayers, teaching, serving others less fortunate than myself, striving toward the example set by 'Abdu'l-Bahá.

A member of the National Spiritual Assembly to whom I had disclosed my circumstances during that special weekend in Wilmette, had cautioned that whatever faced me in prison, the real tests would begin upon my release. I began to understand what she meant. My sincerity as a devotee of the Cause would then be tested. But with the love of Bahá'u'lláh in my heart, the challenge was not overwhelming. Rather, it brought me great joy, for I had learned that the way to demonstrate the truth is simply to strive to be a Bahá'í. Thank God for opening the door that made possible my release from the prison of self.

The Prayer Experiment

by Maureen Sidio

I first heard about the Bahá'í Faith from my older sister. We were raised Roman Catholic, and at age fourteen I started questioning the teachings of the Church. There was just too much that didn't make sense. How could God be a loving Father and still send folks to eternal damnation for missing Mass on Sunday? So I figured I'd take my chances and look around.

I'm one of seven children, and we all started questioning religion at about the same time. My older sister married a Baptist preacher and became a Baptist. I tried that church, but decided it wasn't for me. After I moved to the west coast, I'd get letters from her from time to time. She and her husband had both started seeking and one letter said she'd gone to a meeting and found what we'd been searching for all our lives — the Bahá'í Faith!

About this time, my husband's sister was dating a young Bahá'í. The only thing I knew about the Faith was that they weren't allowed to argue religion, so I egged this poor, zealous Bahá'í into a debate, and managed to get him a little upset. That was good enough for me! I had disproved another religion. By now, I had decided that denominated religions were for the birds.

Then I got another letter from my sister telling me, 'This is *it!*' The fact that *she* could be so impressed with this religion made me curious. We had planned a family reunion in Alabama at this sister's house, and the rest of the kids came from Cleveland to be there. When I arrived, I found out that three or four of my brothers and sisters had become Bahá'ís, but nothing was mentioned about the Faith. I finally asked about it, and they bubbled over. I learned quite a bit that day, but wasn't ready to make a commitment. So my brother gave me his prayer book and encouraged me to try some of the Bahá'í prayers. Underhanded? Maybe, but it worked.

I left, and began saying a few prayers each day. Slowly, I became a happier person, better able to deal with life. After a while, other things took priority and I stopped saying the prayers. I noticed that the quality of life went down. I thought it rather strange that it happened right when I quit saying those prayers. So I got out the old prayer book and started up again. The quality of life went back up. I was not as apt to lose my temper, and could be more tactful, with less stress to myself.

Two weeks went by and I quit saying the prayers again, this time on purpose, to see if there was any correlation. Of

54

course there was, but I wasn't convinced until I'd run the experiment three more times. I decided I'd better give in.

It had been about one year since I'd first heard of the Faith, and it was as if somebody had put a sign on me which said 'Property of Bahá'u'lláh'. I fought it for as long as I could, but they say you cannot frustrate the Will of God. I declared on Bahá'u'lláh's birthday, strictly by coincidence. Now, my mother and six of the seven children in our family are Bahá'ís.

Black Church, White Church

by Mike Sadler

Before I became a Bahá'í, I was a Christian. I felt, however, that Christianity was not teaching what God wanted to be taught. As I looked around my church, I saw all black people. Fifteen yards down the road was an all white church. Fifty yards down the road from that was another church — all white. All the ministers were teaching and preaching the same thing about the coming of Jesus Christ. Why couldn't all these churches get together? I saw hatred and prejudice within the church I attended, and I knew that I had to move on.

Jesus loved everyone without preference for race, creed or color, and these people in the churches were supposedly patterning their lives after Him. Yet the blacks disliked the whites, and the whites disliked the blacks. To me, everyone is human, no matter what color. Now my love for everyone was being challenged by 'Christians'. There had to be something more. I had to search.

I was a senior in college at that point in my life, working part-time in the audio-visual department of the university library. One winter morning, a young lady named Cissie asked for my help. When I wondered why she smiled so much, she explained, 'I'm a Bahá'í.' I had no idea what it was, and little did I realize that it would change my entire life.

We talked about religion and she invited me to a potluck dinner given by the Bahá'ís of Chattanooga. When I entered the room, I felt a warmth and love I had never experienced before. In Cissie I saw the love she had for everyone and a closeness to God.

I began going to many Bahá'í events and became more and more involved with the Bahá'ís, although I wasn't one. I still wore a cross around my neck symbolizing that I was a Christian. I would have become a Bahá'í sooner, but there was one question I had to find the answer to: Was Bahá'u'lláh Who He said He was? The book *Thief in the Night,* being with the Bahá'ís, and much prayer finally answered that question. Six months passed before I realized the truth that was before my eyes. Jesus had already returned. I became a Bahá'í on July 8, 1979, at 1:24 a.m.

In the Clouds of Glory

by Thomas Lysaght

The academic and social pressures of a senior year at Harvard University had thwarted all attempts on my part to incorporate my new belief in God into a lifestyle. It may seem strange for one who had received the benefits of a Jesuit education and had even considered the priesthood as a vocation, to refer to belief in God as a new belief. However, the world's suffering as well as my own had led me, at the age of eighteen, to first deny, then defy, God's existence. I had already been an atheist for three years when, while researching my senior thesis on the English Renaissance poet, George Herbert, I began to believe that yes, there might be a creative force of Intelligence after all.

If I were now to reverse my convictions, I needed to examine the stirrings of this new belief, in solitude, away from the distractions of academia and the rote of routine. At the college graduation ceremony my godmother presented me with a round-trip ticket to Australia, and I knew that the setting for my inner journey had been provided. Away from radios, phone calls, and the busy treadmill that keeps us distant from our selves, I decided I would wrestle with my self on the other side of the world.

In November of 1974, after a summer of traveling throughout the United States, I boarded a plane bound for Australia. Stopping *en route* in Hawaii and Fiji, plunging myself into foreign lands and cultures, with no contacts and little money, I finally arrived in Sydney on November 12, unaware of the significance of the date. I spent the first night in a youth hostel. The following morning, while standing on a bluff overlooking the angry Pacific Ocean, I assessed my situation: forty dollars in my pocket, 10,000 miles from home, and no friends in the entire country. Loneliness engulfed me. Tears filled my eyes and I wished someone would cable me pleading, 'Please come home immediately. We need you.' I was scared, but had come this far for a reason. In my little backpack I carried only three volumes: a Bible, *The Portable Walt Whitman,* and Sri Aurobindo's *The Adventure of Consciousness.* I had chosen them very carefully. With the Bible I would examine prophecy; with Walt Whitman I would celebrate the oneness of all humankind; and with Sri Aurobindo's inspiration I would push my meditation to the point of accomplishing my part in the plan of universal redemption.

I had been given the name of a potential contact in Sydney. Fortunately, this person offered me a job working with opals — those precious stones, 95 per cent of which are found in Australia. I worked in the office suite of the largest opal exporter in the country, and found a room in a respectable boarding house, with a view of Jackson Harbor. After work each day I would catch a ferry across the bay and retire to my room for a simple meal of bread, cheese, and Russian tea. I would then peruse my books, meditate upon their contents, and attempt to pray to the God in Whom I now believed. Over the course of the next two months I felt myself becoming in tune with this Greater Will. Synchronistic events occurred — what many of us call coincidences — that confirmed me on my path and strengthened me in my devotions. I fasted on December 5, the anniversary of Sri Aurobindo's passing, and spent the evening meditating in the city arboretum. All in all, I was pleased with my progress and confirmed in my new belief.

Meanwhile, at the Opal Centre I met scores of miners

who would appear with briefcases, satchels, or carefully tied linen handkerchiefs in which they concealed their precious gems. They would display them, then barter with our three in-house experts. One day a short, squat miner with a thick German accent entered our office. After brief discussion and bargaining, he received a satisfactory price for his handful of opals. Then he sat back with a glass of beer (good will gushing from him) and told stories of the famous, but elusive, black opal. As we talked he took a liking to me, and insisted that I come out to Lightning Ridge to stay with him and his family while investigating the mines. Soon the office would be closed for Christmas week, and this seemed to be a perfect opportunity to witness the mining of those gems with which I had been working for two months. The German miner gave me his address and hurried off, happy with his sale and hoping to reach home before Christmas.

The more I thought about journeying to Lightning Ridge, the more I liked the idea. So a few days before Christmas, with backpack and sleeping bag, I set out for the Australian Outback. My destination was 500 miles inland from Sydney. In 115 degrees heat, I hitchhiked over the Australian wasteland, sleeping at night under the stars. I finally arrived at Lightning Ridge, only to find that the German miner had not really expected me. Not being one to force myself on people, I proceeded to the center of town, namely, the saloon. It bustled every day from nine a.m. until the last drinker stumbled home in the early hours of the morning. In fact, the entire town was what I imagined a town in the old wild American West to have been like. All that went on was drinking, gambling, and whoring. It was quite depressing.

I lingered in the bar, the only haven from the heat, and was soon befriended by a young German fellow. We passed the time together talking. I learned that the conversation going on all around me — miners telling stories of what they had found or hoped to find — was a daily occurrence. The day dragged on, and I wondered where I would spend the night. When no possibilities presented themselves and the cool evening had subdued the blistering heat of the day, my new friend invited me to accompany him to his place. His 'place' was a wrecked automobile on the outskirts of town. It served as both bed and home. When he retired inside, I sat looking at the Pleiades for awhile, then reclined on the back seat of the automobile that had driven us to this spot. Having only a down sleeping bag for bedding in the intense humidity, I alternated throughout the night sweating inside the bag, then lying on top of it — easy prey for the many mosquitoes.

The discomfort of that evening was nothing, however, compared to the turmoil my soul was suffering as I witnessed the way of life in Lightning Ridge. It appeared as if the entire town lived in the tavern. After a few days in this environment, as if through osmosis, the dying quality of the town permeated my being. Without even having dabbled in the decadence, the bottom dropped out of whatever spiritual progress I had managed in Sydney. The fact that it was Christmas time added to the poignancy of the situation, but that was not the essential reason for my depression. I believed in the universal redemption of humankind — that all of us are in this together. Yet the attitudes and activities in Lightning Ridge offered no hope that man is willing to strive toward the betterment of his condition.

My one solace during that sojourn in Lightning Ridge was a café in which food and non-alcoholic beverages were served. It was usually empty. I would retire there during the day either to write or to read, in order to escape the tavern society. It was the one place in town where I felt at peace.

I did a lot of crying one night (Christmas Eve to be exact), as laughter echoed from the saloon and I walked the empty streets alone. That evening I resolved to leave Lightning Ridge, to leave Australia, and to return to my few friends in America who were interested in spiritual transformation. I could not be very strong, I concluded, to have lost everything so easily. I was a candle in the wind. Although at the nadir of my spiritual search, I was not defeated. I simply needed a support group. And I needed it quickly — before my small flame might be extinguished.

The next morning as I sat sipping tea, I overheard three teenagers talking. They were leaving in one hour for Newcastle. They had come to Lightning Ridge on holiday, had drunk themselves silly, and now were going back home. I asked if I could catch a ride with them, and they consented. I threw my few things into the car, gave a hasty farewell to my German friend, and was off. We were less than two minutes on our way when a police car appeared, out of nowhere it seemed, an apparition in the desert. The siren drew us to the side of the road. I exited from the car with my new traveling companions and heard one whisper to another, 'I hope he don't see the heroin.' I was so low, scraping the bottom so sorely at this point, that I didn't even react. Fatalistically, it seemed the logical progression in my state of affairs — to be arrested for possession of heroin. The ultimate absurdity, yet so fitting.

The sheriff threw open the trunk (or boot as the Australians say) and was distracted by the rifles. He demanded permits. Luckily, the teenagers produced them from their wallets. The sheriff created such a fuss over the rifles that he neglected to search the trunk any further, and waved us on. I climbed back into the car, vowing that at the very next town I would take leave of these youths. It was either that, or stand alone at the side of the road in the Australian wasteland where few cars pass each day. We drove on, stopping at every opportunity to shoot at whatever living thing we happened to spy. I endured, but barely.

After an interminable amount of time (probably only half an hour) we pulled into another one-street town. As the tank was being filled with petrol, I picked up my few belongings, stepped quietly from the car, and walked down the wooden sidewalk, never pausing to look back. I had not gone more than a few dozen yards when who should I encounter but a chap I had worked with at the Opal Centre in Sydney. Another one of those coincidences. He was visiting his estranged wife and young daughter, and invited me to accompany him back to the house to spend the remainder of the holiday season. I was saved, at least from worrying about transportation and housing. I wouldn't have to scrounge for survival as I pondered my next move.

I stayed with his family for a few days. In the scorching desert heat, parched to the point of spiritual dehydration, I bided my time. I was simply waiting to get back to Sydney to earn one week's salary to supplement my almost depleted savings. Then I planned to hopscotch from one city to another to utilize my remaining airplane tickets, touching down for a day or two in each town, then moving on. It would be a roundabout way of going home, but I *would* be going home, and would savor that American pilgrimage with an immigrant's devotion.

Returning to Sydney, I returned to work. However, the following week revealed the telltale signs of my descent into Lightning Ridge. It was nearly impossible to pray or meditate. Dashing my New Year's resolution, I returned to imbibing wine to mollify the pain. And I plunged into Henry Miller's *Tropic of Cancer* with the skewed logic that the darker regions had to be traversed and confronted

62

before the light could break. It was a week of unconsciousness, of unmindfulness, of clouded confusion. I had been thrown down to the ground, and before picking myself up, I was going to wallow in the mud for awhile. I wondered if I would ever have the strength to once again begin the slow and arduous process of awakening.

But when Saturday arrived, with eighty dollars in my pocket, a straw hat upon my head, and my duffel bag thrown with the flippancy of a scarf over my shoulder, I was on my way to the airport, singing, 'I'm going where the sun keeps shining/Through the pouring rain . . .' Destination: Canberra, the Capital Territory of Australia. But more important, I was going home. I could feel it in my bones. To this day I can see my reflection in the department store display window as I passed singing — my face was radiant, my gait lively. My soul seemed to sense changes to which my mind was still a stranger.

After an uneventful flight, I disembarked from the plane and wandered around the airport for a few moments. My intention was to hitchhike to Mt. Kosciusko, the highest point in Australia (although only 7,000 feet above sea level). I planned to climb the peak, and hoped there to meditate, pray, and regain the serenity and illumination that had been sucked out of my soul in Lightning Ridge. Before I had time to step from the airport terminal, however, a big, black, bearded, aboriginal gentleman approached me and declared, 'You need a ride.' I am certain it was not a question, rather an assessment of my condition. I paused, stared the stranger in the eye, and nodded my head. 'Wait here one second', he instructed me, and was off.

I watched him approach the luggage carousel and greet two elderly gentlemen who were dressed in western clothing, but who appeared to be East Indian. The party of three

63

then turned and headed in the direction of their car, the aboriginal man motioning for me to follow. At this point, one of the Indian men, weighed down by the burden of his baggage, said something to my new-found chauffeur. All I heard was the reply: 'No, he's not a Bahá'í.'

I virtually stopped in my tracks. It was as if a bell had pealed in my head. 'Bahá'í.' It sounded so distinct. Immediately, that old sense of synchronicity, that feeling of coincidence which had been so strong in Sydney, returned. 'This is not a coincidence', an inner voice seemed to be instructing me. 'Investigate this.'

I followed my new friends to the car and we climbed in. Conversation was minimal. There was none of that uncomfortable chatter that strains to bridge the chasm that yawns between us all. However I wanted an answer to my question. I wanted to know what Bahá'í was. My bearded friend replied succinctly, but I don't recall what he said. He did mention that a Bahá'í youth conference was convening that day in Canberra at the university, and that these gentlemen had come to participate. My curiosity went unsatisfied.

As we drove on, although usually oblivious to the passing countryside, I could not take my eyes off the clouds that had formed in the sky. I had never before seen such beautiful formations. Strewn across the vault of the heavens were strands of ribbon clouds, and miles below them, in bold relief, stood large, white, puffy cumulus clouds — herds of white buffalo nosing through the sky. The effect was breathtaking. Although in an unfamiliar situation, with strangers, and with many questions to ask, I kept my head halfway out the window.

'Where is it you're heading?' the aboriginal gentleman inquired.

'Oh, I don't know. I thought maybe I'd hitchhike up to

Mt. Kosciusko.'

There was a pause. 'If you haven't any place to stay, you can stay at my house if you like. Of course I can't promise you a bed. There will be many people arriving, but you're welcome to throw your sleeping bag on the floor.'

I hesitated. No, I did not really hesitate. The feeling that this encounter was not a coincidence was too strong. I merely paused, lest I appear too anxious. 'Okay, thanks.'

The matter was settled. After a few miles we reached the university and the other two gentlemen departed, having uttered hardly a word the entire drive. My host and I continued in silence. I was happy to have the opportunity to observe the beauty of the clouds without interruption.

We arrived at his home and I was introduced to his wife. In the living room there were a number of people milling about who had just arrived, having driven from various parts of the continent. There was little formal ceremony of introduction. In fact, what struck me most upon entering was how invisible I was allowed to feel. I was not ignored, or treated inhospitably. On the contrary, I was greeted with courtesy and graciously served a meal. Yet there was a complete absence of that discomfort displayed by people who are unaccustomed to having guests, or of that performance put on by hosts who assume you need to be entertained. Nobody was overly concerned that a stranger had walked into the house. Nobody even seemed to realize that I was a stranger. I was completely at ease.

In time, I was engaged in conversation by a young American fellow, not much older than myself. Few of the others took notice, as they were busy carrying luggage in and out, or arranging who would sleep where later that night. This young man was more responsive when I inquired as to the meaning and significance of Bahá'í. He replied patiently to all my questions. Yet, in my pride,

I was skeptical. I was well-versed in Eastern religions. If Bahá'u'lláh was a major religious figure, why had I not heard of Him? Bart explained a little more. I gestured toward a photograph. 'Is that Bahá'u'lláh?'

'No, that's His Son,' he replied. "Abdu'l-Bahá.'

By this time we were sitting at the dining room table, partaking of the cold meat and bread that our host, Harry Penrith, had graciously and unobtrusively spread for us. 'But if you believe that everything is one, then why do you have to join a group?' I challenged. 'Why do you have to join something to believe in something?' My belief had always been that groups excluded some people and were therefore elitist and sectarian. Bart attempted to reply, but I was too filled with my own questions.

'And what about reincarnation?' 'And how does all this relate to the reality of Jesus Christ?' This was an ironic question coming from me, who only recently in my meditations in Sydney, had come to believe that Jesus Christ was more than a holy man, but actually a Personage Who came at a pivotal point in history.

Bart referred me to a few books, wisely noting that we were both too tired to converse any further. I accepted a volume entitled *Thief in the Night*. But traces of doubt still lingered in my mind. I judged Bart as being a bit too happy for his own good. He had that effervescent quality that was anathema in dispassionate academia, and I was but a recent refugee from university.

People went about their business. Some were now departing for the conference. I was invited to accompany them that evening to a social gathering of the Bahá'ís at the college. I accepted the invitation, and meanwhile found a comfortable chair to relax in, noting how trusting it was of them to leave me alone in the house.

I began to read. The author of the book, William Sears,

66

had gathered all the Biblical references to the Promised One, to Christ's Second Coming, and had scientifically set out to pinpoint where, when, and how this messianic event would take place. I had not read very far, however, when the beauty of nature overcame my attachment to the printed word. I arose, approached the window, and gazed once again at the clouds in the sky.

That evening I accompanied some of the Bahá'ís to the get-together at the university. As I looked around at the diversity in the crowd — old, young, black, white, rich, poor, educated, illiterate — I realized I had never before seen any group, religious or secular, displaying such diversity. In addition, I noted their sincerity. Something kept repeating itself over and over again in my head as I watched the Bahá'ís interacting, something the Romans used to say: 'See how these Christians love one another.' A sincere, heartfelt love was visible. I was witnessing not only a veritable cross-section of humanity, but one in which the members were obviously comfortable in each other's company. I was deeply impressed.

The next morning upon awakening I immediately went to the window and looked up at the sky. The clouds were still in formation, ribbon clouds across the vault of the heavens and cumulus clouds miles below. I joined my new friends in the kitchen for breakfast. Most of the Bahá'ís had planned to return to the university that morning for workshops and talks. The daytime sessions were for Bahá'ís only, and rather than embarrass them with pointed questions as to why this was so, I simply stated that if no one objected, I would remain in the house most of the day reading.

After they had gone I picked up *Thief in the Night,* but had not read for very long when I was driven to the window once again to look at the clouds. I then returned to my seat to read what was proving to be a most engaging book. After a number of strolls to the window, I finally decided to step outside. I wanted to be near those clouds. I lay face down on the front lawn and continued to read, but soon rolled over on my back, enraptured by the clouds. As I read, I came to a passage where the author quotes Jesus Christ, 'And then shall they see the Son of man coming in the clouds with great power and glory' (Mark 13:26). The book dropped from my hands. I felt a presence. I looked up and realized that He *had* come again, in the clouds of glory, as Bahá'u'lláh.

That Sunday afternoon was my first inkling that I had been pulled out of the mud of Lightning Ridge. On Monday night, I attended an informal fireside where a man named Joe talked about the Faith. He said little that enforced my mind. I knew in my heart already. As he spoke, the question entered my mind: 'If I turn from this, where then shall I turn?' I knew that night, January 13, 1975, that I was a Bahá'í. The few intellectual objections I had at this point would not be an obstacle to the intuitive, emotional, heartfelt awareness that the rest of my being, my soul, possessed. But I did not declare my belief in Bahá'u'lláh that night. I still had many questions.

I spent the rest of the week reading *The Seven Valleys and The Four Valleys* and *The Kitáb-i-Íqán*. I went to the university every day to read beside the river or to walk with Ian Reid, a thirteen-year-old boy who had befriended me. In his youth there was a relaxed, quiet quality that appealed to me. He was comfortable with the teachings of Bahá'u'lláh, and had nothing to prove or push. So to Ian I put my questions. We walked and talked, and as I listened I would look upon him and think of Christ, at the age of thirteen, teaching the elders in the Temple.

On Thursday night, the last evening of the conference, I

enrolled in the ranks of Bahá'u'lláh's followers. I was embraced and welcomed by many, including the Hand of the Cause of God, Collis Featherstone. I also learned that there were Bahá'ís living in Lightning Ridge, and that these Bahá'ís owned a café — the café to which I would retreat from the spiritual squalor while I sojourned in that mining town. So the little peace that I had found in Lightning Ridge had been provided by Bahá'u'lláh. He had been watching over me all along.

After the conference I continued my journey to the major cities of Australia. In each town I looked up the Bahá'ís (the new friends I had met in Canberra) and saw that there really are Bahá'ís living the teachings of Bahá'u'lláh. Departing from Australia, stopping in New Zealand and Tahiti, finding Bahá'ís everywhere, I realized that this is a universal Cause. I had found the means toward universal redemption.

The Album Jacket

by Susan Strong

I had never heard of the Bahá'í Faith and was, or so I thought, quite satisfied with my own religion, when I happened to buy the Seals and Crofts record album 'Summer Breeze'. I have always been curious by nature, and there were certain lyrics to a number of the songs that whet my curiosity. I was particularly taken with '... be lions roaring in the forest of knowledge, whales swimming in the ocean of life', and was determined to try to locate the full passage from which it was excerpted. Asterisks from the different passages on the album jacket kept refering me to 'Bahá'í Scriptures'.

I made a point of going to the local library during my lunch hour, and obtained a copy of *Bahá'u'lláh and the New Era*, knowing only that it was a Bahá'í publication. It was a book I couldn't put down. I read it every spare moment in the evenings. As a child in a parochial school, I had often asked questions during religious instruction which had the routine responses of 'Because the Bible says so', and 'You must have faith'. The *New Era* was answering those questions I had long since filed away!

A written inscription indicated the book had been donated to the library by a local Bahá'í group. Upon returning the book, I questioned the librarian about the donors but was told it would be against regulations to divulge individual names. I was asked to return in three days, when the supervisor would be available. Perhaps she could provide the information. Three days later I queried the head librarian, getting the same response. However, this woman 'happened' to have a daughter whose best friend was a Bahá'í, and she would be glad to give me that telephone number.

With some trepidation, I made the phone call to a perfect stranger. The woman on the phone seemed genuinely pleased to hear from me and invited me to lunch the next day. Her warmth and apparent sincerity during our luncheon visit made me feel I had known her for years. We kept in touch and exactly one month after my visit to the library, on Naw-Rúz, I declared my belief in Bahá'u'lláh — beginning a new year with a new life.

Cranking the Ditto

by Niki L. Glanz

The year was 1972 and my life was a microcosm of the travails of American society at that time. For the past several years I had been employed as a teacher in a large midwestern high school. The school had an outstanding academic reputation, recently having been ranked as No. 1 in the United States. But what attracted me to it was its amazing diversity of races and cultures. Situated in a multiethnic suburb near Chicago, the school had blacks, whites, hispanics and students from more than thirty different foreign countries, as well as all the social classes from near-ghetto to upper-upper. The chance to experience the unity of mankind while working and learning seemed like paradise.

Yet my dreams soon became shambles. Rather than being a source of joy and growth, the school's diversity became a cause of dissension and disorder. Blacks versus whites, blacks versus hispanics, old versus young, conservatives versus liberals — all with the concomitant verbal and physical violence of those years. As a social studies teacher my classes also became embroiled in the issues of the day: the racial problem, agitation over the Viet Nam war, the drug issue, and dissatisfaction with the prevailing materialistic culture. For me there was no escaping modern America's dilemmas. Yet try as I might, I could find no real solutions.

Various committees were formed to consult on the school's problems, but these too seemed to fracture over the monumental issues before us. The school's academic standing began to plummet and the community itself, of which my husband and I were members, seemed close to chaos. I remember thinking that maybe man alone could not solve these problems.

Individually I could think of only one solution: work harder. Although I became pregnant in the late fall, my thoughts were not on my child-to-be, but rather on my job. Early in the morning, late at night, Sundays, constantly I worked, hoping somehow my efforts would abate the school's problems. If anything, the extra work was counter-productive, making me only more tired, irritable and unhappy. In this frame of mind I first received the message that was to change my life and my view of society forever.

As I now remember, it was a Tuesday or Thursday in February, about 7.30 in the morning. I was in the teachers' workroom, running off yet more ditto copies for yet another intricate lesson plan, when another teacher arrived for the same purpose. As we cranked the ditto machine we commiserated: Oh, how tired we were; oh, how the students didn't appreciate our efforts; on and on. My fellow teacher, an edge in her voice, complained, 'And last night I couldn't get to sleep. These Bahá'ís downstairs kept me awake so long!' I had never heard of Bahá'ís and my mind conjured up all kinds of images. I asked with a bit of trepidation, 'Bahá'ís, what do *they* do?' The teacher responded angrily, 'They laugh! They laughed so much I couldn't sleep.' Laugh? Someone in this world is so happy that they keep upstairs neighbors awake by laughing? I was stunned! It was as if someone had thrown cold water on my face. I stopped cranking the ditto machine and stood still for several moments.

Though I had now heard of the Bahá'í Faith, it was still some time before I investigated it. School ended in June. I was retiring to have my baby and meanwhile to write a textbook on politics for junior colleges. My mind had been

72

so preoccupied for so long that the birth of my daughter Joy on August 11 came as a real shock. She was beautiful! She was a real, live, darling baby I could hold, love and nurture. The true beauty of life, which for so long had eluded me, somehow became omnipresent with her birth.

Yet though she was big and beautiful, there seemed to be something wrong. She never really woke up and I could barely get her to nurse. When I asked the doctors about it in the hospital, they assured me that she was just tired from her birth exertions and would soon snap out of it. But at home there was no change. One morning, after a week at home, I noticed Joy's rib cage protruding markedly and suddenly realized my child was dangerously ill. I rushed to the pediatrician's office.

He took one look at her and literally tore across the street to the community hospital, cradling Joy in his arms. I ran after them, dragging my trench coat behind me. We dashed up the stairs to the children's ward where a team of neonatal experts was hastily assembled. I sat in the hallway outside the door where people rushed in and out to work on my daughter. At one point the pediatrician approached me and indicated there was very little hope. Joy's body weight had dropped too drastically to support her life systems, he said. I was in a stupor. The beauty that had come so suddenly into my life was now just as suddenly being removed.

I remember thinking, 'I should pray'. But I had been away from religion and God for so long, I was unable to. Instead I rushed to the bathroom, sobbing and heart-broken. Finally I emerged to resume my post by the door when a young woman approached me. She and her husband, whose daughter also lay in the hospital very ill, had seen what had happened and wanted me to know that they had prayed for us. I was dumbfounded! Here God had answered the need of my heart, despite my own frailties.

It was several days before we knew if Joy would survive. The doctors isolated a virus that had entered through her navel, but the real cause of her illness was never determined. When she finally began to recuperate, I made a solemn promise: never again would I let myself be so distant from God that I could not even pray for my dying daughter. For her sake, and mine, I would find out the truth about God and His creation.

Once Joy was back home again, I determined to do just that. I knew it was religion I was seeking, in fact, from my experiences at school as well as with my daughter, I was craving religion. But I wanted it to be true religion. Although I loved Christ very much, His Church appeared to leave out too much of humanity. For that reason I turned away from Christianity.

I picked up the Yellow Pages, about to turn to 'Religions', and mentally reviewed others I had heard of. Zen Buddhism? Probably interesting, but a Zen Buddhist art professor I had known did not seem at peace. Bahá'í? Yes, possibly. After that morning in the teachers' workroom, some friends had told me that another teacher at school and her husband were Bahá'ís. This had greatly astonished me as they had never mentioned their religion, despite the fact that we were good social friends. I liked them very much and so decided, 'Why not? I'll call them up and invite them over to expain what the Bahá'í Faith is.'

We were all quite nervous on the telephone but the meeting was arranged. Somehow in the US of 1972, and especially among our social circles, religion was taboo. So I decided that I would have to be discreet about the hunger of my soul for Truth. I arranged for my friends to sit on two chairs opposite a sofa where I had carefully placed a tiny notecard with my questions and concerns in minuscule handwriting. As we talked I surreptitiously glanced at the card, making sure that all the subjects had been covered. Relation of religion to science. Equality of women and men. Unity of different cultures. View of other religions. Peace in the world. Finally my teacher friend commented, 'These questions sound like the basic principles of the Bahá'í Faith!'

Indeed, all that my heart and mind had been seeking for so many years was enshrined in this beautiful Faith. Though encouraged and excited, I was determined not to rush into something as important as religion. Instead I began attending firesides, informal discussions about the Bahá'í Faith, in a nearby home. The hosts were Persians and here I had to confront the charge that I was 'getting mixed up with some strange Eastern cult'. Their love, kindness and patience, plus the beauty of the teachings themselves, quickly dispelled such fears. Finally I had to confront deeper issues — the possible hostility of my family at my accepting a 'new religion' and the possible estrangement of my husband and our friends who were not interested in religion.

One day my teacher friend called to see how I was progressing in my investigation. When I voiced these reservations, she responded simply and earnestly, 'Oh, Niki, you can be a Bahá'í!' She was right. Before anything else one must find God. In February, just a year after hearing about those people who laugh, I formally entered the Faith. Several years later, God bestowed upon me the additional gift of a son, Gregory. Together he, Joy and I have experienced a happiness that is impossible to describe. May we continue in this path with the utmost thankfulness and enable others to also experience the beauty of becoming a Bahá'í.

A Seminarian's Vow

by Paul Provost

As a Catholic priest serving in the ghetto areas of Water-bury, Connecticut, I had little desire to search for new activities or ideas. With increasing frequency, however, I questioned the religious beliefs which had originally moti-vated me, and the answers seemed more and more inadequate. Consequently, I traveled to North Carolina to speak with the priest who had been my spiritual advisor, and decided that I could no longer continue in the ministry of the Roman Catholic Church.

My introduction to the Bahá'í Faith came two days later. On the return trip to Connecticut, I stopped to visit a cousin in Pennsylvania. At dinner, we discussed my decision to leave the priesthood, and she suggested that I speak with her neighbor, who had just become a Bahá'í. Although the Bahá'í had recently broken an engagement to be married, she remained very happy. Maybe she could help *me* out? I consented, but not enthusiastically. At this, my cousin called her neighbor to explain the situation, and when I arrived, I was treated to a private fireside by a beautiful Bahá'í. I thought everything she said was very nice for her, but wanted to know when I would get my chance to talk. We called a truce, listened to Nina Simone records, fell in love, and ten months later we were married. But not before I was exposed to further firesides and zealous new believers who managed to turn me off almost completely.

After nine years of firesides, deepenings, slide shows, work weekends at Green Acre Bahá'í School, and potluck dinners, I finally became more than intellectually interested in the Faith. Questions would come to mind and as each was answered, another obstacle was eliminated. The book *Some Answered Questions* provided much assistance during this period. The final obstacle proved to be Muḥammad. For almost two months, I spent all my spare time researching the Qur'án, the Bible, Bahá'í Writings, and secular literature, trying to eliminate the prejudice which had been taught me about this Manifestation.

On August 14, 1979, I took my oldest son to a movie at the local Episcopal Church. As I anticipated a delay at the start, plus several reel changes, I asked my wife for a book to read. She handed me *The Proclamation of Bahá'u'lláh*, and I read intermittently, 'O Concourse of Christians! ...' 'O Concourse of priests! Leave the bells ...' 'O Concourse of monks! ... Enter ye into wedlock, that after you someone may fill your place.'

Having three beautiful children, I was reminded of the first time I read those words, under very different conditions, ten years earlier. My reaction then was, 'Who is this with the power to eradicate the concept of the vow of celibacy?' But that didn't matter any more. When I returned home, I was ready to declare my belief in Bahá'u'lláh, which I did on August 15. The date was significant since, for five years as a seminarian, I had pledged vows of poverty, chastity and obedience on that same date. Now I understood why.

Handicap

by Emily Lee Phillips

My mother and grandmother were both Bahá'ís, so I grew up with the full force of Bahá'u'lláh's earthshaking teachings behind me. Although I had the unusual bounty of having a Bahá'í parent, it took a chain of events to prompt me into enrolling in the Faith at the age of twenty-five.

There was one other special feature to my childhood: my falling victim to polio in the 1953 epidemic. My legs were paralyzed by the disease, and I spent the years between the ages of five and twelve learning to walk no less than six times. I was flattened by surgery for months at a stretch, forced to relearn the ambulatory process after every bout in the operating room.

I am sure Bahá'u'lláh's guiding hand was with us. My doctor was one of the few physicians in the world who liked to work with polio patients, and to teach families to train the victims (usually children) to be independent in spite of the handicap. His name was David Grice. He denied me a wheelchair, insisted my mobility would be limited until I was willing to use leg braces and crutches, and teased me often. One day I saw my chance for getting back at him. In a room full of doctors, he told me to give him 'a big kick', so I did, and he laughed heartily. The new braces were working.

Being raised as a Bahá'í was not easy, especially in the little town of Pembroke, Massachusetts. So much time went into explaining to my peers what the new religion was all about, that I began to wonder if my mother and grandmother were the only Bahá'ís in the world. I also had to get used to my nickname, the 'Beehive Kid'. Then my father set himself against organized religion in the belief that it did more harm than good in the world. My mother decided to withdraw from the Faith rather than cause family friction. This never dampened her love for Bahá'u'lláh, fortunately, and she taught my brother and me to say Bahá'í prayers from an early age.

Mother's Bahá'í friends lived far away during most of my childhood, and by the time I reached college age during the tumultuous sixties she had completely lost touch with them. In my heart I believed I would one day become a Bahá'í, but the fact that I never encountered any Bahá'ís was a definite factor in my slowness to join the Faith.

In 1966, I left my rural hometown for the enormous college conglomerate of Boston University, where I studied journalism. Despite the large size of the Bahá'í community in Boston and the surrounding area, I met no Bahá'ís in my four years there. Of course, I never thought of hunting through the phone book for listings, nor did I conduct any methodical search for members of the Faith. Still, I wondered if they were out there. The truth was that I did not feel compelled to align myself with a religion (I was having a great time checking into several other disciplines, including meditation), so the absence of Bahá'ís seemed a confirmation that I was not ready for the Faith.

At the end of my senior year there were no graduation exercises, because violence had erupted in Boston in response to the National Guard shooting of several Kent State University students during an anti-war protest, causing BU authorities to cancel the ceremony. Several days before my 'paper graduation', my brother was killed in a violent, fiery auto crash. The effect this had on me was tremendous, but the significant action to come out of the shock and sorrow was a serious study of Bahá'í teachings. Those relating to life after death were especially appealing.

79

Once I had satisfied myself that my brother was still alive in the Abhá Kingdom, and that his soul would continue to progress partly as a result of prayers and good deeds offered in his memory, my interest expanded. I knew I was ready for the Bahá'í Faith at that point, but the lack of Bahá'í contacts prevented any progress.

Inevitably, other activities claimed my interest. I learned to drive, went to work as a news reporter, bought a sports car, and began to take an interest in civic affairs. I was out to prove that having a handicap is no barrier to leading a full life. Still, the longing for something much bigger than myself and my circle of activities haunted me.

Four years after my brother's death, Mother was inspired to write to some Bahá'ís she had known twenty years earlier. She told them of my interest in the Faith. These friends, Ethelinda and Harry Merson of Falmouth, Massachusetts, responded by inviting me to a fireside. I set out on the hour-long drive in the highest of spirits, at the end of March, 1974. Awaiting me in Falmouth was perhaps the oddest fireside I have ever attended. A non-Bahá'í Chinese geologist told us about his work in Australia. I felt right at home with the Bahá'ís gathered in the Merson home, and loved every minute of the event. The room seemed to be filled with a golden glow.

A week later I went back for a second, smaller fireside, at which several Bahá'í ladies were present. We had a pleasant evening, reading and talking. I felt so comfortable that I wasn't even mildly surprised when Ethelinda asked if I were ready to enroll in the Faith. 'I don't see why not', I responded. (New Englanders generally don't get excited about the biggest events of life.) I didn't know all the Bahá'í laws I was supposed to abide by, but that didn't matter. I read over what was written on the declaration card, said to myself that whatever laws Bahá'u'lláh had established were just fine with me, and signed without another moment's delay. I had made the single most important decision of my life.

What a joyous time it was at that fireside! I could barely restrain my excitement, but finally it grew so late that I had to leave. The car sailed home by itself. With immense effort I resisted the urge to shout the great news to my soundly sleeping parents. I contented myself with opening the new copy of the *Kitáb-i-Íqán* which Ethelinda had presented to me, and began reading at 2 a.m. In so few hours I had become a member of the 'Army of Light' which Bahá'u'lláh refers to, and in my joy I thought I understood exactly what the term meant.

Seasons of the Soul

by Margot Johnson

Years ago, in a small Methodist parsonage, I came rushing into this strange world, restless, eager and very much afraid. During my entire childhood, I was aware of ever trying to adjust myself to this peculiar world but seemed always unable to do so.

At the age of five, a playmate of mine was found dead in bed, having eaten some poisoned candy. This, to my already fearful self, was an awful blow. Sleep simply could not be indulged in, for if I closed my eyes, perhaps the same fate awaited me. Night followed night of endless terror, of vainly trying to hold my eyelids open, of terrible pictures of being buried in the ground. My terror was only enhanced

81

by having to say my evening prayer, 'Now I lay me down to sleep ... If I should die ...' I didn't want to die, and pictures of angels and heaven held no interest for me. All I knew was that I wanted to escape death, but sensed in my childish way that escape would come only from finding God. And so my search began.

At the age of six, I joined the church much against my father's will, as he thought me too young to understand. I indignantly insisted that I did understand, however, and as I was able to answer all the questions as well as my older brothers could, he allowed me to join with them.

This did not give me the relief I sought, for I still was afraid of the dark, of death, of everything. It seems as if my childhood was full of terrors from which my parents tried in vain to free me. One terror after another showed its ugly head, and when I tell you that for six long years I never closed my eyes at night without the fear of death being present, you can know it was very real. And so from the first I knew great terror and great hunger for relief.

As I grew, there were other things to fight as well. I began more and more to question. Even in childhood, I did not feel that the Protestant churches held all the truth. I doubted much that was taught me and often pained and surprised my patient father with my long and doubting questions.

I could feel no joy because of the atonement. I was told that Christ died to save me from my sins, yet I didn't seem to be saved from them. I could not make things fit together. It all seemed so vague, so unreal. If I expressed these feelings, I saw shocked faces and was thought irreverent.

At the age of twelve, I decided to become a Catholic. I was allowed to go to Mass, and the service inspired me with a reverence which heretofore I had had very little of. The picturing of some of the mysteries helped to make them mine. Although very much impressed, I did not find all that I sought. I yearned to worship. I longed to know God, but could not find in the orthodox system anything which held or comforted me. I always prayed and almost always had guidance. Still I found no peace.

About this time a great tragedy occurred in our family. My brother, through overwork in college, had a nervous breakdown and after a severe case of brain fever, lost his mind. My precious brother, only sixteen, so gifted, so handsome, afflicted in this way. Poor Daddy and Mother, who had sacrificed so much for God and who had lived their belief so beautifully, so simply, stricken with this terrible blow. I was numb, speechless with rage at a God who would strike us like that. I refused to pray, decided to turn my back forever on all religion. From that time forth, I would believe nothing.

Never shall I forget those prayers of faith and pain that ascended from our family altar. Never shall I forget the anguish in Daddy's voice when he prayed, 'Not our will, but Thine.' Not so, my feeling. I had simply turned to stone. But God heard my mother's and father's prayers, and one day when all seemed hopeless, when even the finest specialists said my brother could neither live nor be healed, his mind cleared and his reason returned. God had performed a miracle. My brother was healed!

It is hard even now to speak of that time, but two things had been made very clear to me. A miracle had been performed, and my parents had a love for God which even a blow like that could not shake. Their faith had been rewarded. Still, what they believed did not satisfy me. They had an inner nearness to God that I seemed unable to feel.

Aside from my own precious father and mother, I saw so few who seemed to have even a spark of the thing I longed for. Most of them were too self-righteous or had such an anemic sort of goodness that they aroused in me nothing but contempt, and their prayers rising to heaven did nothing but anger me.

While inwardly all this turmoil was going on, outwardly I was the minister's daughter, the target of the whole town, the object of every criticism. Because of the suffering this brought me, I sought in every possible way to shock the good brethren and sisters and to live up to their wildest predictions. Oh, little girl of long ago, early indeed did you learn how few are the understanding hearts. How little did these people know what a bleeding heart you hid under your proud and daring defiance.

At the age of fifteen I became very fond of a boy several years my senior. We used to spend long hours together questioning about God, yearning for His meeting, the boy already having known some close communion. One day he gave me a book to read called *In Tune with the Infinite*. I sat reading. All at once I was caught up in a great whiteness. I sat still, but my spirit soared to great heights. I was immersed in a flood of light, divinely happy. The whole world was changed — people, things were no more to be feared. I could even think calmly of death. I looked down and saw the realities of all things. It was heavenly, beautiful, and lasted about three days. Then darkness closed in again. That same summer I met a Christian Scientist. She tried to show me how to overcome fear, and although she did help some, I could not regain the glory I had experienced.

Years passed. I went to Denver and met the man whom I married. His mother, seeing what a fearful creature I was, sought to help by interesting me in New Thought. I went to many classes and received much assistance. I even seemed to be able to leave my body at times, but it did not satisfy.

One day all alone in the Rockies, far from any human

being, as I gazed about me at the mountains so tall and mighty and at the peaceful valleys, and thought of how God made Himself known through all His handiwork, I heard a voice say, 'See this little cloud. See how trustingly it floats in this great azure sky. Some day when you lay aside your body, you too will float, in God's great ocean of love.' At last it was gone forever — that terror of death, that fear. I knew that when death came I could trustingly lie in the great arms of God and sleep.

About this time, a great and terrible grief drove me far from God. Perhaps nothing is so wrecking to a woman's whole being as the disillusionments which sometimes come in marriage. The rainbow gleams of my girlhood dreams were things of long ago, and if heaven did hold all for which I had sighed, I wanted none of it. I never prayed. I defied. But the longing would not be allayed and after terrible anguish, I again began my search, seeking exactly what, I did not know, but feeling sure that I would some day find what my soul cried out for.

Again I tried New Thought, but it left me feeling dead, inert. The pressure became so great I could hardly endure it. Night after night I paced the floor. I believed there was an answer to all this hunger and begged and implored that I might find it. One day as I sat listening to a New Thought lecture, hungering and yet finding nothing to satisfy that hunger, I heard a voice again. 'There is no more light here for you. Go to the Bahá'í library.'

I had read a few things in the Bahá'í literature before, but nothing had seemed to open for me. Still, I heeded the voice. Never shall I forget the night I crossed that threshold. I didn't hear the speaker. I didn't see the people. Again I was caught up on a high mountain. Again the earth was naught. At last I was home. I felt like a tired wanderer who had finally returned to his abode. I was numb to all the earth. My body went through the motions, but I was soaring far from the face of man and gazing into the Face of the Eternal One.

So divine, so holy, so great was the celestial joy, how can I describe it save to say that all the terror, all the anguish, all the pain of all my life, I would have endured gladly for one hour of such heavenly light. It was so still, so majestic. I was the fleecy cloud floating in God's heaven of blue. At last I had found my answer. I knew that I had opened the door of my soul and it was seeing the dawn of a new day.

After many weeks this great ecstasy began to subside. Then came the questions. How did I know? What could I prove? I pored over the Bahá'í books and almost as fast as came the questions, there were the blessed answers. A rational proof of the existence of God. How precious that was to me, so simple yet so clear. How my heart cried out in praise and thanksgiving when I found it! Science and religion could and should agree. The other religions of the world had also been right. God had sent His messengers to them as well as to us. The surprise and wonder at the Tablets of Bahá'u'lláh and 'Abdu'l-Bahá! Many times as a question that had bothered me came to mind, I would hasten to the books, and it seemed as if an unseen hand would open them to the very page and verse that held the answer.

This was the day of God's great Revelation to man! I longed to shout it from the housetops. The Lord of Hosts, He is the King of Glory! At last I had found Him. Now I knew why I had searched, why passages in the Bible had seemed like words of fire. For this had I hungered, for this had I longed. A new heaven and a new earth were mine.

Then one night in a dream I was told the next step I must take. I shrank back in anger and despair. But had I not said I was willing to pay any price for what I yearned to find? Aflame with this new message, aching to share it, never was

86

a task more difficult than to return to my parents, only to be refused a hearing. I felt lifeless, dead. Yet I sensed dimly that I had to be broken before He could fill me with His divine grace.

After several months of seeming winter of soul, one very dear to my heart came to me in great need. Bahá'u'lláh poured light and help through me to this dear one. When after two long months of struggle this wound was healed, God took me again to a high mountain. One of His perfect mirrors, one of His chosen messengers came to me, and with such gentleness, love and selflessness became the guide who took me to still greater heights, to the Inner Sanctuary, to the Holy of Holies, to the very Throne of God.

How can words ever tell of the grandeur of that celestial glory? I stood as one breathless before the Throne. What mattered all the pain and sorrow? Oh! to be melted and lost forever in that great ocean, to become one with that limitless sea. Oh Glory of Glories, to think that at last my eyes have beheld Thy splendor and my ears have heard Thy voice! Thine, oh Bahá'u'lláh, my Lord! And the friendships! When I try to tell of my beloved ones, those to whom I have come so close, who can speak this language of the heart, words fail me. I used to wonder what the communion of saints meant; now it is so clear. That dear friend who held me steadfast by his prayers and words of encouragement in those first days. The letters that brought light and help in those first months. The one who brought me Tablets to read and who made Haifa and 'Abdu'l-Bahá so real to me. The precious meetings where some of the friends fairly glistened with joy and beauty. The one of humble heart whose letters and manuscript sent me flying up to heaven in sheer ecstasy. And that radiant one, I tremble as I write of her, so surrounded with the Glory, so saintlike in her beauty. All of these dear ones have come to me as precious angels from the celestial world, to guide me, to love me. No more am I alone. This is the love of God which passeth all understanding.

That I, so unworthy, so sinful, should receive this divine privilege, I prostrate myself before the sacred threshold and in anguish beg to be made pure, patient, humble, fit for my Master's use. If one so sinful, so disobedient as I , can enter His Presence, there is indeed life and hope for the whole world.

> In the nest of Thy loving kindness,
> Amid the branches of the tree of Spirit,
> This bird, featherless, broken-winged,
> Has found her abiding-place.
> Praise, Glory, Dominion and Power
> Are Thine, now and forevermore.

Party Circuit

by Barry Wootten

I emerged from the partying side of society. There came a time when the need to evaluate my actions was at hand. Actually, it was an ongoing evaluation with constantly negative results. But failure to take action brought me to an all-time physical and mental low.

Drugs and alcohol were a large part of the problem and they had to become a thing of the past if any progress was to be made. Medical help was needed for the ulcer which had found its way into my stomach. Also, my chain of friends had to change from the large circle of partying people, to a small circle of those who could relate to straightening out their lives and trying to more deeply understand things.

Pulling away from that party atmosphere and dealing with poor physical and emotional health were a lot to handle all at once. It was *change* that was difficult. Casting aside the familiar for the unfamiliar is scary. After past attempts at stepping out of the familiar and repeatedly falling back, I now felt stronger to face and deal with the upcoming indescribable emptiness and directionlessness. The slowing down of partying took place over a period of many months. I gradually stopped using drugs and alcohol, found new friends, and obtained help for the ulcer.

Work was also difficult. I had been appointed Assistant Manager of a wholesale warehouse, but due to the total disorganization and near bankruptcy of the company, I wasn't very happy there. The wall to climb seemed beyond the clouds.

One of the representatives of the products we sold came in weekly, and this man always seemed to be happy. He was very friendly and stopped to talk with my fellow workers as time permitted. One day after he left, a couple of my friends began to tell me about the Bahá'í Faith. They had been discussing it with him, and were impressed. I thought it seemed mildly interesting, but focusing thought on anything was hard for me. Though I had always believed in God, church was a thing of childhood. Most of my encounters with religion had been with the forceful approach which had totally turned me off.

One of my friends was particularly interested in going to a Bahá'í meeting, called a fireside, to learn more about this religion. She tried to get me to go but didn't force it, and went without me. She was aware of my present state of being, and after the fireside was even more convinced that I should go. She told me what she had learned, and it began to seem more interesting.

Through her efforts I was present at the next fireside. No one there forcefully approached me. That was worth examining in itself. These people were friendly, very friendly. The things they talked about made sense. Everything about the Bahá'í Faith fit together like a puzzle. They made me feel extremely welcome, extending an obviously heartfelt invitation to stop by any time.

The Bahá'í Faith wasn't a mysterious religion that I was unable to relate to. In fact, it wasn't religion as I had pictured it at all. It seemed more real, something that anyone could tap into at any level and have access to immeasurable knowledge and progress. Though it was obvious that there were many things to become aware of, the tools to build a more fruitful life were clearly in the Bahá'í Faith. Three months of investigating came to an end with my declaration of belief in Bahá'u'lláh

Fightin' Word

by Lisa Paulson

The word 'Bahá'í' has been around my family for as long as I can remember, but it was a 'fightin' word,' an unspoken word with mysteriously dark and evil connotations. My step-brother, eight years my senior, became a Bahá'í when I was ten, and his father had been a Bahá'í since before my birth. Their religion was never discussed, but when the word had to be used, it was not with favor.

When I was sixteen, I grew openly discontented with the Episcopal Church. I was tired of the 'car wash procedure' as I called it, where the congregation was regularly pronounced dirty and in need of cleansing by the prayer books and ministers, lined up, and washed of sins in communion, to emerge sparkling clean until the next Sunday. I attended other churches to see if they were any better, but was not happy with any, though I believed in God and in Christ. I entered Doane College in Crete, Nebraska (population 4,444), when I was seventeen, and continued my search, with little luck.

Home for Thanksgiving that year (1976), I met a Bahá'í from Albuquerque, New Mexico. It seemed that her home, her smile, her life, were filled with the wisdom, happiness and laughter I so desired.

I saw my brother that Christmas, and drew him aside to tell him of my unfruitful search. He listened carefully, in a manner I had long respected, and then gently said, 'I can't tell you what you should believe in; all I can do is share with you what I know.' I agreed, and accepted his gift of *Paris Talks* by 'Abdu'l-Bahá. This book was equivalent to contraband in my household, so I hid it until I got to Crete. When I had free time I sat down and started to read.

The introduction answered some of my basic questions, as no factual information had been given to me in eighteen years of hearing the word 'Bahá'í'. Then I turned to the first page and read 'Abdu'l-Bahá's first sentence: 'When a man turns his face to God he finds sunshine everywhere.' I felt as if a huge water-like store of frustrations, hopes, prayers, and anxieties was released. I knew instantly that whatever 'Abdu'l-Bahá said was what I believed. My search was over and I could grow and be happy like the other Bahá'ís I knew.

I obtained the number of a Bahá'í in Crete, called, and

91

the woman who answered invited me to a gathering at her house. I walked to her home that Sunday, January 9, 1977, and found another loving, listening Bahá'í. Noticing there was no one else there, I inquired about the others who were expected and was told they were *en route*. I asked a few more questions, then said, 'I guess I came here to become a Bahá'í.'

She was somewhat taken aback, but carefully explained the process of signing the membership card and meeting with representatives of the Local Spiritual Assembly. She also told me about the Bahá'í laws. In the course of our conversation she had determined what I knew of the Faith and at this point she visibly hesitated. Nevertheless, she got a card and had me read the statement of belief. While I was signing it, her husband and two other believers arrived. 'We have a new Bahá'í!' my hostess announced, and all four of them welcomed me into the Faith.

Two weeks later, I met with the Local Spiritual Assembly representatives, then caught a plane to New Mexico for a wedding. My parents would be there and I was wondering how to tell them. I didn't really know why they were so opposed to the Faith, as I had seen nothing to indicate that it deserved harsh treatment. When I arrived in Albuquerque, I saw my brother and the Bahá'í I had met during Thanksgiving, who had first shown me her wonderful life. We exulted about the specialness of the Faith and my becoming a part of its swelling ranks. I decided that night was the time to tell my parents.

They absolutely hit the roof. My father said I had to stop my membership in the Faith or he would withdraw all financial support. My mother yelled at me. I cried, not understanding their reaction.

The next morning, I called the woman who had enrolled me, explained what had happened, and told her to hold my

92

membership card. She was sympathetic and did so. I never stopped meeting with the Bahá'ís when I could, or telling other people about my search. 'I'm not a Bahá'í, but I've been checking it out, and I think it's really great,' I'd say to people on the plane, at college, or in town.

In my reading of the Bahá'í Writings, I learned that while Bahá'u'lláh emphasizes the importance of family unity and obedience to parents, He also teaches that personal investigation and declaring one's faith are important. I struggled with this, and explained to my parents that I would respect their feelings by agreeing to investigate other religions, which I tried to do in tiny Crete.

In January of 1978, I met with the Local Spiritual Assembly of Crete to discuss my being enrolled. I wanted to fully identify myself with the thing that gave direction and light to my life. In a letter to my parents I wrote, 'After a year of trying to show you that *I love you* and will always love you, and respect your beliefs, I have come to the conclusion that you will not really believe my love unless I completely renounce the Bahá'í Faith and Bahá'u'lláh. This I will not and cannot do.'

After meeting with the Spiritual Assembly of Lincoln, Nebraska, where I had moved to attend the university, I was enrolled on January 9, 1978, exactly one year from my declaration in Crete. The relief I felt was similar to that when I read *Paris Talks*. At last I could call myself a Bahá'í without adding, 'But I'm not enrolled'. I could contribute to the Funds; I could go to Feast; I could attend those so-special Bahá'í-only conferences. I was prepared to tell my parents of my action and accept all consequences.

Premonition in Saigon

by Karen Jentz

I became a Bahá'í in the spring of 1975, at the exact time of the ending of the United States' political involvement in Viet Nam. I had previously worked in the US towards the ending of the war, and was in Viet Nam in April 1975, working in a nursery where children were salvaged from orphanages and streets, fattened up, and sent to new families overseas.

As the pressures of life in Saigon became extreme, I no longer knew where my energies belonged, and felt an overwhelming urge to leave the country at all costs. Not comprehending, I obeyed the inner voice, telling those that I worked with only that I had to leave, and arranged to take a convoy of eight babies to Montreal. This mission accomplished, I decided to try to find some peace in North Carolina, where my parents had recently moved.

The evening of my arrival, we watched the news in horror, as pictures of the children I had been caring for in Saigon only a week ago flashed across the screen. The plane which was to transport them to the first home many would have known in their lives, crashed shortly after takeoff, and many were killed. Had I remained in Viet Nam I would have been among them. The faith in God which had sustained me during the long months in Viet Nam, was not tested, but faith in myself, in being able to act consistently and responsibility, was. I felt that I had run out on the children, and could find no peace for the anguish in my soul.

Then I spotted an ad for a Bahá'í meeting in a nearby town. The featured speaker was Dr James Turpin, who prior to becoming a Bahá'í had established several medical hospitals in Viet Nam. I was drawn by the fact that he, who so thoroughly knew the wrenching conditions that were tearing my own heart apart, could be addressing himself to a religion, and not to the purely social and humanitarian issues which seemed so pressing to me. I didn't hear much of what was said at the meeting, but afterwards, as I went to talk to the speaker, I encountered a Bahá'í who had declared his faith in Viet Nam. Through recounting his experiences, he turned my attention from Viet Nam to the Bahá'í Faith itself. I attended a couple of firesides, visited his family on the Cherokee Indian Reservation, and declared my faith in Bahá'u'lláh two weeks after that first meeting.

I had discovered that the goals of my previous humanitarian and political work were sure to be realized through the Bahá'í Faith. Instead of the slow salvage work which I had been doing, there was an already evolving *new* World Order which I could become a part of.

Trumpet Blast

by Gary Kugler

My first real spiritual awakening occurred during my freshman year of college at the University of California at Santa Barbara. A good friend became a fundamentalist Christian and he got me interested in the spirit of Christianity — as opposed to the form of it. I asked Jesus to come into my heart and to help me live a good life. I read the New Testament from cover to cover, since I wanted to know as much as possible about my new faith.

The group that I became more or less a part of was non-denominational, because we felt that all Christians should be one. I never became totally involved, however, because even though I responded to the message of Christ, I didn't like the fact that Christians interpreted the Bible in different ways. I had trouble with the notion that if something in the Bible were not clear, I should just pray and would receive the answer. How could they explain that when different people sought an answer to the same question through prayer, they would receive conflicting answers? I also realized that there were many paradoxes, and that there was no plan of action to solve the world's problems. The Christians were just praising God, while waiting for Jesus to come down on the clouds and solve our problems for us.

I was really in noman's land. I wasn't considered too rational by my non-religious friends and wasn't truly a part of any group of Christians. Feeling desperate, I went to my favorite place overlooking the ocean, to talk to God (if He really existed). I cried bitter, hot tears, and told Christ that I believed in Him but didn't know what to do, as I suspected was truly the case with all Christians. I wondered if I was failing to see something that was obvious to those whose faith in Christ was so strong. You can imagine how heart-wrenching it was to feel that Christianity, the only hope for the world, was in such a state of confusion. I really felt burned. My prayer to Christ was something like this: 'I pray that You will lead me to follow You in the way that You want me to. I will wait and see what happens. If nothing ever happens, then I will know that faith in You is a waste of time.'

Thus, Christ and I had a clean break. I didn't bother to pray after that. I went back to living in a way that was un-befitting a Christian. However, I had my eyes and ears open and did not criticize anyone for following Christ.

About one and a half years later, I met the girl who was to become my wife. Eileen was a turned-off Catholic by the time we met. We quickly became close friends. I told her everything concerning my spiritual quest. We agreed that we believed in God and Christ, but didn't know what to do about it. We made two half-hearted attempts to go to church together to see if there might be a denomination acceptable to both of us. Absolute failure!

A few weeks before we were to marry, Eileen attended a professional meeting and met Kate, a young woman who had just become a Bahá'í. Kate was very friendly and invited us over to her house for dessert and to hear about the Bahá'í Faith. Eileen thought she and I could agree on this Faith, but I wasn't interested in any 'new religion' and especially didn't want to get burned again. It would be nice to meet a friendly person, though. We didn't have time to go to Kate's house before the wedding, but two months later, through persistent efforts, Kate reached us at our new address and again invited us to hear about the Bahá'í Faith.

We had a great dinner at her house during which no mention was made of religion. What patience on her part! Then she asked us if we wanted to hear about her new Faith. Sure, why not. She asked if we were Christians, and when we explained that we were confused Christians, she dropped the bomb that Christ had come again. This was incredible to me! (Eileen wasn't too fazed because she, as a Catholic, wasn't really expecting Him to return anyway.) I asked Kate to explain how this could have happened without the signs mentioned in the Bible: trumpet blasts, riding on the clouds, the end of the earth, and so on. Being a new Bahá'í she couldn't explain these very well, so she invited us to a large fireside in her community.

After that night at Kate's, Eileen and I decided that this

97

was probably just another one of the many false religions that were cropping up. After all, if this were truly the return of Christ, why had we never heard of it before, and why did it have so few followers? For months we didn't bother to read the introductory material Kate had given us.

Again, we were invited to a fireside. We weren't enthusiastic about the Faith, but liked Kate, so we went. It was a good fireside which opened the avenues of questioning. I had many questions relating to Christ's return. I wasn't at all convinced at that meeting, but my curiosity was aroused. We returned home with a stack of books to read, and in a few months, Eileen and I were ready to become Bahá'ís.

From Mauritius With Love

by Carolyn L. Hansen

As seniors in high school, each of us was expected to write a term paper. My essay explored various religious and philosophical answers to the question: Why is there pain and suffering in the world? The explanation which made most sense to me was found via the index of a Bahá'í book. So exciting was this answer that I sought more information at the public library in Bexley, Ohio.

In a book on comparative religion, there was a section on the Bahá'í Faith, with impressive pictures of all kinds of people associating harmoniously. As I read the list of basic social principles of the Faith, I thought, 'Why, I agree with every single one of them. But then, I'm perfectly happy as a Disciple of Christ.'

From another book I learned that the Bahá'í Faith had been founded a little over a hundred years ago, so the circumstances of its beginning were better documented and its sacred writings more authentic than those of other major religions. Fascinating. But the term paper deadline called me away from pursuing this path.

Two years later, as a pre-ministerial major at Bethany College in West Virginia, I did some reading in the *Millenial Harbinger,* and felt sorry for the errors made by Alexander Campbell and others in predicting the return of Christ in 1844. (I had quite forgotten reading just two years earlier about the declaration of the Báb in May 1844.) During summer schools in Illinois and Louisiana, I was attracted by posters advertising firesides. 'What's a fireside?' I wondered, on the run to my next class. 'The Bahá'í Faith is something I have to look into sometime.'

Following graduation and marriage, my husband Tom and I moved around a lot. As Episcopalians in South Dakota, Maryland, and Mississippi during the tumultuous first half of the 1960s, we were proud to be part of a religious force for positive change. In the fall of 1965, in Nashua, New Hampshire, we joined the community chorus — and met our first Bahá'í.

During the next couple of years, we kept running into Ray and Mary Elliot around town. Although there was a racial difference between us, we felt more comfortable with the Elliots than with anyone else in Nashua, and seriously considered moving next door to them.

When one of my students at the Catholic college where I taught asked for ideas about an unusual term paper she could write for another professor, I suggested the Bahá'í Faith, inviting Ray Elliot and Boyd Leavitt (chairman of the Nashua Spiritual Assembly) to answer her questions about the social teachings of Bahá'u'lláh.

Sometime later, Ray asked if he and Mary could bring over something they thought we'd be interested in. As an historian, however, my husband could out-argue the charts on socio-religious history which they brought to share with us. Despite all this contact, neither Tom nor I felt the Bahá'ís to be more than nice people to know.

Since coming to Nashua, we had not been entirely happy with the Episcopal Church. Due to the extremely rapid growth of the city, it seemed that every church service contained an appeal for more in the collection plate so a larger building could be erected. Such appeals turned us off. The final straw came when it was decided to cancel our favorite ceremony of the year: the Christmas Eve midnight celebration. This seemed hypocritical, as some of those agitating for the cancellation might stay out until 2 a.m. drinking in a popular night club.

Defiantly, we attended the midnight service at an Episcopal church in a nearby town. Later we joined that church, but felt it never became a meaningful part of our lives. In fact, by apple blossom and lilac time, the car seemed to just drive right by it. In August, I attended communion alone at another church and was startled to hear an interior voice state firmly, 'You have just had your final Episcopal communion.' 'How ridiculous,' I answered. 'I'm just looking for the right congregation. I don't want to quit being an Episcopalian.'

In early September, I noticed a small item on the back page of the newspaper, announcing that a man from Mauritius would be speaking at the home of Ray and Mary Elliot on Saturday night. 'Let's go!' I said to Tom. 'When else would we ever have the chance to hear someone from Mauritius speak? And we haven't seen the Elliots in ages.' But he was uninterested, so I went alone.

Ray was surprised when he answered the door: 'Never

thought we'd see *you* here!' Gradually the room filled with people, the final arrivals having been called at home to bring their own folding chairs. The guest speaker was late coming up from Boston, but the two dozen people assembled did not seem to mind. I marveled at how interesting the conversation was. Here were people who had ideas about lots of subjects, who talked about more than just their own children, and who didn't complain about jobs or the state of the world. They genuinely enjoyed being together — without alcoholic beverages, which surprised me.

Finally the speaker arrived. He looked around the room, asked if there were many non-Bahá'ís present, and whether he should give a general introduction to the Faith or address himself primarily to the Bahá'ís. The only non-Bahá'í there, other than myself, was married to a Bahá'í, so I urged him to please talk about specifics. I was impressed that here was someone coming from a little-known, third world nation to teach about the Faith — quite different from the US sending missionaries to the Congo or Korea, different even from having clergy come to speak about the churches in their native South Africa or India. It was startling to learn that this man would work in a hospital laboratory until he had earned enough money to travel to another country in order to teach the Faith.

But most of all, I was impressed by his explanation of how the Faith had united the diverse Bahá'ís of Mauritius. How people who had belonged to various Hindu castes in their native India now ate together in Mauritius. How they also shared their table with Bahá'ís of Muslim background (Hindus and Muslims had long been arch-enemies). How local Assemblies also included Bahá'ís of French Catholic background and of African animistic upbringing. How this great diversity of peoples were trusted, and were often

101

appointed to governmental positions on that small island in the Indian Ocean.

Then our speaker told how he had been invited to speak to a Black Muslim group in Cincinnati, and to the John Birch Society in Atlanta. As one who had lived through some very frightening and frustrating times in the South, and who was distressed over the recent assassinations of Martin Luther King and Robert Kennedy, I was definitely intrigued. But at one point, the speaker said something disparaging about social scientists. 'Does that mean I'd have to quit being a sociologist if I became a Bahá'í?' Everyone looked startled (probably most of all me, because I had not consciously thought about such a possibility), but assured me that there were few occupations which would cause problems for members of the Faith.

The next day, I phoned the Elliots and said I might be interested in becoming a Bahá'í. Did they have anything I could read? They left a copy of *Bahá'u'lláh and the New Era* in their mailbox for me, and I read it in one day — in between cleaning bouts, after I read that Bahá'ís must be neat and clean. That evening I called the Elliots again, and asked when the next meeting was.

They must have arranged it just for me, at the Leavitt home, for only Mary, the Leavitts, and Sandy and LaVerne Rhode were there. The latter two impressed me greatly, for it is unusual to see a mother and daughter truly listen to and respect each other's opinion. That evening was devoted to the Bahá'ís answering the many questions which I had scrawled in the margins of *Bahá'u'lláh and the New Era*. Eagerly I went to the Rhode home the following night for another fireside.

After that I attended Bahá'í functions wherever they could be found. I even dragged my husband to a picnic clear up at New Found Lake, as well as to Green Acre

Bahá'í School in Eliot, Maine. At a fireside in Maine given by Dwight Allen, then a member of the National Spiritual Assembly, again I witnessed a rare affinity between parent and child. Being a very busy man, Dwight was rarely able to spend much time with each child, so he had brought along a young son, who perched happily on his dad's armchair, reading his own book when he wished and listening intently to the conversation when it interested him.

Finally, LaVerne asked me when I was going to declare. When she explained that I shouldn't wait for Tom because it was an individual decision, I met with the Spiritual Assembly of Nashua and became a Bahá'í on October 16, 1968 — twelve years after picking up a Bahá'í book in the public library in Bexley, Ohio.

Kansas Farm Boy

by Duane L. Herrmann

I grew up on a farm outside Topeka, Kansas, and to people in Topeka we lived in the sticks. We were a devout Lutheran family. There was no question about it. As soon as I was old enough to go, my grandmother took me to Sunday School. While my class was being held, she taught one herself, continuing until she was nearly eighty.

Looking back, I can see threads where the Bahá'í Faith had been indirectly woven into my life. During the long winter evenings we would beg our father to show the family movies. We had each Christmas, each birthday, and other momentous events on film. One movie was of a trip that a group of farm wives, including my mother and

103

grandmother, took to see Chicago. The tour stopped briefly at the Bahá'í House of Worship. Since 1953 the House of Worship had been in our family movies—but no one knew what it was.

I remember coming home from church some Sundays and watching the last bit of an interesting TV show. We only saw the last few minutes and then a man would sweep the credits off the screen with a broom. Years later, when I read *God Loves Laughter*, I learned more about the mysterious show. It was Bill Sears' 'In the Park'.

While I was in junior high school, the Topeka Assembly placed a booth in the local fair. I was drawn to the pictures of the Houses of Worship. They looked religious, but they weren't churches! I didn't recognize the name Bahá'í and wanted to learn about it, but being a shy farm boy, I ran away from the kind old lady sitting in the booth.

The two family farms were next to each other, and before I went to school, I would walk across the pasture to 'Gramma's'. Our relationship deepened as I grew, and naturally we talked about religion. On summer nights we would stay up past midnight talking. We were sure the end of the world was near and that Jesus was on His way. Gramma didn't always agree with the church (sometimes I was surprised at how much she disagreed), but she believed in Jesus. She also told me so much about her life and family that I feel I have lived the entire century.

In the seventh and eighth grades I became fascinated with past civilizations and their beliefs. They didn't have the Bible, since they lived before Jesus. Would God really condemn them for living in the wrong time? And what about the books which had been excluded from the Bible? Who decided they were no longer holy? I decided to find those 'lost' books to determine for myself if they were the Word of God. I also wanted to study the Holy Books of

104

other religions. Why should someone decide for me that Buddha was a heathen? Or Zoroaster?

In my Lutheran confirmation class the minister of the family church explained that after confirmation each of us would be responsible for our own spiritual education as adults. That was all I needed. I took him at his word and began to study all the religions I could. In Sunday school I had learned a lot of Jewish history but nothing of other religions, and wanted to make up for lost time.

In high school I began to build my library, and read the Apocrypha, the *Book of Mormon, Worlds in Collision,* and other books. While continuing my religious education, I did not neglect church activities. I ushered and taught Sunday school for four years, was elected president of the youth group, and twice wrote the children's Christmas program. I was a 'good' boy and did the 'right' things.

The dichotomy between my actions and beliefs didn't bother me since I considered myself a liberal unorthodox Christian. With that label, I felt all right about my actions. As an usher, I could slip away from the service relatively unnoticed and go to a deserted room in the basement for my own service. When the organ began, I returned upstairs and finished ushering. I could do my thing and theirs too.

The minister was set against any alteration in the order of the service. He would not even allow one youth Sunday a year. I kept my feelings more and more to myself, began listening to the Radio Church of God, and stopped taking communion. When I read the Church Constitution one Sunday, I realized that I didn't believe those things at all.

The Radio Church of God was heavy on the imminent return of Jesus, and my grandmother and I fully believed it would happen soon. I would lie awake at night, fearful that I would be 'asleep' and miss Him when He came. My most fervent prayer was not to miss Jesus.

105

In my senior year, the instructor of my speed-reading class told us to obtain books on a topic we were interested in. I bought my first books on the occult, and reading them was a journey into a fascinating world I had always hoped existed. That year my horizons were expanded out of this world! I willed myself to see auras, anticipate events, and interpret dreams, and fancied inventorying past lives.

The summer after high school I enrolled in a college class, Composition I. It was taught by a Bahá'í. This was the turning point. My papers and his comments made for a running conversation which ran right to the Faith! He invited me to a fireside, and of course I went.

At the fireside, I saw the photo of the House of Worship and fell in love with it. And I was amazed by the people. I knew, from the moment I entered the house, that this little group had something special, and I wanted to be part of it. For the first time in my life I felt treated like an individual. The Bahá'ís were interested in me (not my family, or school, but me!) and accepted me for what I was at that moment. But no one inquired if I wanted to join and I was too shy to ask. They simply kept inviting me back, and I kept going.

I learned a lot in the next six months. I took three versions of the Bible and a Bible dictionary, and discovered for myself that Jesus taught that Heaven and Hell were conditions, not places. I learned the meanings of several puzzling dreams of long standing. I let go of the occult. With no transportation, I couldn't go to the family church, but visited the ones nearby and became aware of the similarities among Christian churches.

Prior to the first Bahá'í Week in Topeka, in November 1969, I was sent a list of the week's activities. Some weren't too interesting, but there was to be a free meal. Poverty-stricken at the time, that appealed to me. I talked my landlady into going so I could have a ride. Following this dinner for the Birth of Bahá'u'lláh, the film 'A New Wind' was shown. I didn't want the movie to end. When a Bahá'í offered me a ride to see it a second time, I accepted.

Before the second showing, I was invited to dinner with a few Bahá'ís — an evening I will remember for the rest of my life. The spirit and laughter were more nourishing and memorable than the delicious food. The stories this warm and loving group of friends exchanged gave a whole new meaning to 'family' and 'community'. God was getting me ready.

I don't remember the movie. I don't remember the talk or the discussion that followed. But as we left the building, a Bahá'í from another town, who had seen me once at a fireside, waved from a distance and called out, 'Good-bye, Duane'. I was stunned! She remembered my name! I was barely a fleeting insignificant acquaintance, but she remembered my name!

My mind did not stop whirling. Later that night in bed, I carefully examined what the Bahá'ís believed and what I personally believed. Point by point I went over what I knew, and was a bit surprised to find how many of our beliefs matched. I realized that if I were not to be a hypocrite, then I was unquestionably a Bahá'í. I had no choice. I wasn't forced. No one was with me or knew what I was thinking. I believed what the Bahá'ís believed — therefore I was a Bahá'í.

Little did I anticipate the effects of my logical and reasonable conclusion. Some people rock the family boat — I think I sank mine. One uncle acted as if I were a fire-breathing dragon about to devour his children, and once nearly threw me out of his house. My aunts were sure my soul was on its way to Hell. My mother still refuses to say Bahá'í correctly. And I broke my grandmother's heart.

Religion is seldom talked about when I'm around.

Over the years, however, the situation has improved a great deal. My uncle stayed home from church to watch 'And His Name Shall Be One' on TV. He feels I have become a nearly normal person, especially since I've gotten married and become a father. An aunt has begun asking about the Bahá'í trips I take. My mother adores her grandchildren. My grandmother and I looked at *Bahá'í World, Vol. XIV,* page by page. She was impressed by the pictures of so many different kinds of people, who seemed so happy; she was outraged at the destruction of the House of Worship in 'Ishqábád. And nine years after I began going to firesides, my brother embraced the Cause of God.

In Desperation

by Elaine Shevin

It was rare that I had a happy day in my married life. My relationship with my husband was one of constant turmoil and aggravation. One night, after a particularly stormy session, I found myself unable to sleep. My muscles were tense, my heart was pounding, my brain refused to calm down — reliving the evening's arguments over and over. By 2 a.m. I was worn out.

I had never been one to depend on faith and was not much of a believer in God, but on this particular morning, I could stand it no longer. In desperation I turned to the Lord. 'I want to believe. I need something strong to hold on to and depend on. If you really exist, can't you give me some kind of sign?' I pleaded over and over.

Suddenly I started shaking violently and my right arm

shot out rigidly as I lay on the bed. I felt as if an outer force had total control over me. I was at once frightened and excited. Then the feeling was gone. I drew my arm back to its normal position and thought about what had happened. I knew I was not asleep. Was this a sign or just some weird muscle spasm? I began to doubt that it had even occurred. 'Oh God,' I pleaded in silence, 'If this *was* the sign, please repeat it just once so I'll know it really happened. I'll never ask for another sign or doubt your existence again.'

I waited. It was so still. Suddenly my arm stiffened as before and stretched upward, as if pointing to something far beyond my comprehension. A radiant light shone in upon me, coming out of a totally black sky on a dark night. I began to cry uncontrollably, the tears running down my cheeks and onto the sheets below. When there were no tears left, a feeling of total peace settled over me. I seemed to have a direct line to the whole universe. There was no earthly interference. I knew utter bliss and deep, deep joy. At that moment, the ray of light drew away, far into space and beyond, and it was once again dark and still in my room.

'I believe, I believe!' I cried with great joy. It was more than just a belief in the existence of God. I had been aware of the Bahá'í Faith through the interest of my daughter, and now, without question, this was the path that I wanted to follow. I ran to the next room where my daughter was sleeping, and with tears in my eyes, told her why I had to wake her up. Quietly, she said she had just been praying that I would see the light. At the next Bahá'í fireside in my locale, I declared my faith.

Mind and Heart

by Randie Gottlieb

I was a suntanned California girl with a slight greenish tint
to my waist-length blond hair, the result of hours spent in
chlorinated water teaching swimming. The most important things in life were volleyball (I was trying out for the
US National Team), wood design (my major in college),
and boys — or rather one in particular. The thought of God
never entered my mind.

In 1970, while backpacking alone through Europe with
my youth hostel card and railpass, enjoying one last adventure before settling into the domestic routines of marriage,
I received a letter from my boyfriend Steve, announcing
that he had just become a Bahá'í.

Being unfamiliar with the word, I questioned my fellow
travelers in the Amsterdam youth hostel where I was stay-
ing for the night. Piecing together the various bits of
information that were offered, I concluded that Bahá'ís
were weird religious fanatics who shaved their heads,
peddled incense, and chanted on street corners. Poor
Steve! It was hard to accept that one so brilliant, one who
had earned straight 'A's throughout high school and been
elected class valedictorian, could have fallen so far. My
plans for marriage were canceled immediately.

Several proposals later, I realized that I was still in love
with Steve, and decided to return home to knock some
sense into his misguided head. I arrived in Los Angeles
and was surprised to find that he was acting like a normal
human being. And he still had all his hair! For months I
ignored his patient attempts to introduce me to his new-
found Faith. Although he never pressured me, I could feel

how important it was to him, and I knew that sooner or later he would have to make a decision. Impatient, I forced the question: 'Who do you love more, me or God?' 'God', the answer came back without hesitation. I was crushed.

There was no choice left but to read the Bahá'í Writings in order to disprove his Faith. Steve would surely come to his senses when he realized the errors and contradictions they contained! I went through fifteen Bahá'í books in a systematic manner, carefully noting prophecies, checking dates, and verifying historical facts at the local library. My investigation left me furious! Not only were there no contradictions, but everything fit together. The Bahá'í Faith was logical! It made sense! How could I possibly talk him out of it? I was really angry now.

The next step was to read the holy books of other religions. After all, I wanted to be fair. I studied Buddhist scripture, the Old Testament, the Bhagavad Gita, the Christian Bible, and the Qur'án, as well as the Book of Mormon, and the tracts of Jehovah's Witnesses, Adventists, vegetarians, chanters, meditators, 'Moonies', and other groups. I enrolled in a comparative religions class at my university and attended a retreat for born-again Christians with a friend.

Meanwhile, my parents had become quite upset. My mother couldn't understand what I was searching for with such zeal — especially when it aggravated my father so. My father tore up Bahá'í books, cursed Bahá'u'lláh's name (which he pronounced 'Bahoo-LaBoob'), and made a special point of observing the Jewish holy days, a practice our family had long since abandoned. In order to continue my studies it was necessary to read at night, under the bedcovers, with a flashlight.

Little by little, the words of Bahá'u'lláh were having an effect. One night when I opened *The Hidden Words* and read, 'O Son of Man! Wert thou to speed through the immensity of space and traverse the expanse of heaven, yet thou wouldst find no rest save in submission to Our command and humbleness before Our Face,' I knew it was the Voice of God.

But I didn't believe in God! Yet how could a human being write with such authority? It seemed impossible to really know for sure. Then in 'Abdu'l-Bahá's Tablet to the Swiss psychologist, Dr Forel, I found rational proofs of the existence of a Supreme Being, and I knew intellectually that the Bahá'í Faith was true. But I couldn't surrender my heart.

'O Son of Love!' Bahá'u'lláh seemed to be speaking directly to me, 'Thou art but one step away from the glorious heights above ... Take thou one pace and with the next advance into the immortal realm . . .' Still, I just couldn't commit myself — couldn't take that final step of faith. I wrestled with my indecision for months, rebelling against what I knew was inevitable. If an occasional smile replaced the almost permanent frown on my face, I quickly wiped it off. Steve, unable to help me, could only laugh at my distress.

Finally, late one night, frustrated and at the end of hope, I did something I had never done before. I prayed. 'O God,' my silent words were choked with tears, 'I may never see the light, but if you do exist and if the Bahá'í Faith is really true, the least you can do is let my mother know.'

A minute later she was in my room. 'Randie, wake up! You won't believe what just happened. I hardly believe it myself! I was lying in bed when the room filled with a beautiful light and a clear voice inside me said that the Bahá'í Faith was true! I don't know any of the Bahá'í teachings, but I believe, and I want to be a Bahá'í!' It was a shock, to say the least. My prayer had been answered immediately. God was listening.

The next evening, I drove over to a nearby fireside. My mother was already there. She signed her enrollment card and left. Wonderful. My mother was now a Bahá'í. *I* was the one with all the knowledge, but *she* had the faith. Still, I was afraid to make that final commitment. I wanted more proof.

Just then, a man in the audience began to badger the speaker. Every time a Bahá'í principle was stated, this gentleman took offense and argued why it could not be so. Here was my opportunity. I had found another test for God. 'If that man becomes a Bahá'í tonight,' I vowed, 'then I will too.' Let God try to find a way out of that one. The speaker mentioned another Bahá'í teaching and the attacker jumped to his feet, shaking his fist and shouting. I felt pretty secure at that point. 'I've had it with you Bahá'ís!' he roared. 'You have an answer for everything I say. It's obvious I can't fight you so I might as well join you.' He declared his belief in Bahá'u'lláh.

It was useless to protest any longer. My father arrived at the fireside and marched in to save me just as I was signing my name to the enrollment card. At that moment, all the burdens of my search, all the frustration, doubt and uncertainty vanished. My heart had accepted the new Message and I was filled with light and joy.

The California Connection

by Michael

This story begins in Cleveland, Ohio, where I was going to school and studying drama. I was making my living through what you might call a dealership. In other words, I was a dealer. That is, I used to sell drugs. A pusher. And I was quite good at it. I had an apartment on the top of Cedar Hill, with my roommate Swamp, and our home was a universal home. We had everybody in that house from the dregs of downtown who were heroin addicts off the street, to petty thieves and killers, up to lawyers and policemen and firemen and doctors. Really, it was amazing! My house was like a flower garden. Incredible!

About this time I decided, along with my dear friend Swamp, that I would take a summer off and do a workshop in music and dramatic arts in London. Following that, we would go to Morocco, and send small packages back to the United States, to our dear friends in the business. I figured I'd job in at different plays here and there, you know, enjoy my career as an actor, while making a fortune by sending small packages back to this lovely set-up in Cleveland.

So we left for Europe. We spent the summer at the drama workshop, which turned out to be quite a bore for me. On our way to Morocco we stopped in Spain. I'd been stationed there in the service for three years, and it was like coming home. I love Spain.

One day, while we were walking down the main street in Madrid, I was seized with a fantastic fear! A voice inside told me not to go to Morocco, that it would be terribly dangerous, and that I should return to my folks' home in California. I had never had such an experience, and I wasn't high at the time. It was a cold, sober voice. There was no question. I was terrified! Even when I had done hallucinogens, I always knew what was going on. I'd see different things happening in the room, but I'd know they weren't really happening. This was totally different! I was petrified! (From that moment on, I never touched any drugs.) I turned to my friend and said, 'Swamp, we're not going to Morocco. I'm going home.' He was shocked, really flipped out. I mean, I had set up the whole thing and funded the trip. He was just coming along for the ride, having a good time, and was going to be rich too. But there was nothing he could do about it 'cause I was the bankroll. So we went back to the States.

Back in Cleveland, I found out that all my contacts had been busted while I was in Spain. Had I gone to Morocco, I'd have wound up in jail. That was in 1972.

Before heading out to California, I met a cousin who was really into Guru Maharaji. My cousin was very dedicated and invited me to a retreat somewhere in Pennsylvania. Well, why not. I went and was struck by the deep sincerity of the Guru's followers, but I couldn't help feeling that it was a con job.

While they were doing their different devotional things, I sat down and read the Bhagavad Gita. I had never seen it, never heard of it, never read it. But I fell in love with it! It was the most beautiful book I'd ever read. I realized that this was from God. Between this book and that voice in Madrid, I didn't quite know what was happening, but I knew I was going through a transformation. I wasn't going to run out and shave my head or anything, but I knew that the Bhagavad Gita was true.

After a couple of days there, I came back and was really turned on to start looking for something, or at least be open to what anybody else had to say. A few days later, I ran into an old girlfriend of another cousin of mine. She was Jewish and had gone to Israel at the same time I went to London. While in Israel, she had become a Christian, a really turned-on Christian! I mean, I saw a physical difference in this woman! There was a glow just emanating from her! She said, 'Michael, you have *got* to read the New Testament. It is the Word of God!' She was really insistent about it. You know, Christ was something you didn't mention in our house as a child, let alone bring in a New Testament. But I could see a change in her, so I figured there must be something there. I took it, and — Wow! — I fell in love with it after the first few pages, and read the whole book cover to cover. 'Lord! This is beautiful! Where have you been?'

Then I read the Revelation of St. John. Oh, my God! I realized that we were living it! It was so obvious to me! You know the hundred-pound stones that fell from the air — they were bombs! He didn't know what bombs were. And when he talked about the flaming chariots crashing into each other, he didn't know what Pintos and Omegas were. It was the revelation of *this day!* So I came to the conclusion that there were only three possibilities. Either Christ had come and we missed Him. (I was a Jew and we were known for that, right?) Or He was walking on Earth at this moment. Or He was going to come any minute.

Knowing only those three possibilities I prayed, 'God, please help me. Show me the way.' (I had never prayed before.) I read the New Testament over and over again. And I prayed every day, 'Please Christ, guide me to your new self.' I knew He wouldn't be called Christ. Intuitively, I knew. Then that voice again prompted me to get out to California. I'd heard it before, and decided to go. I wasn't going to mess around.

First I went to Madison, Wisconsin, to see this heart of my heart who I'd met on my famous trip to London. I was

116

going to tell her all about Christ and His return, and how we would both search for Him. I realized real quick that she wasn't at all interested in this weirdo who had transformed in the past couple of weeks. So I left.

I started hitchhiking, and a van pulled up with California plates. 'Wow! You're going to California!' When I got in the car they said, 'Yeah, we're going to California, but it might take us a couple of months. You're welcome to travel with us for as long as you like.' About thirty seconds after being in the car, I started telling them about the fact that Christ had returned, or He was going to return, or He was around here somewhere. The only thing I could talk about at that time was the return of Christ. I was a real pleasure to be around.

There were three people in the van: a man, his wife, and this other gal who was traveling with them. The guy was just into toking on the old smoke, and his wife was a devout Christian who really didn't approve of her husband smoking grass. The other woman was a Bahá'í. So I started talking to her about the return of Christ.

'You know,' I said, 'the Bhagavad Gita, the Old Testament, and the New Testament — it's all the same thing. There's only one God, right? And there's only one religion of God.'

She was sitting there agreeing with everything, and probably thinking, 'We've got a hot one here, man!' She said, 'I have a book for you that I think you'd really enjoy!'

'Sure, everybody in the world's got a book for me, but I've got the only one I need — the New Testament. Thank you very much.'

We traveled about a hundred miles to the guy's aunt's house in northern Illinois, and stayed there a week. He and his wife slept in the house, the Bahá'í gal stayed in the van, and I slept in the garage. We had these long discussions,

117

and every once in a while she'd say, 'You know, I have this book I think you'd enjoy reading.' 'No way do I want your book!'

Well, after a week of traveling from the garage to the bathroom, I wasn't getting any closer to California, so I thanked them and told them I had to leave. They dropped me off at the highway and as I was getting out of the van, the Bahá'í just *stuffed* the book at me. '*Please* take it!' I didn't want to hurt her feelings so I took the book, thanked her very much, and stuck the thing at the bottom of my backpack. Just what I needed. I'm looking for the return of Christ, and some kook's giving me a book. I figured I'd read it when everything else in the world was gone.

I arrived in Madison late that evening and needed a place to sleep. So I went to this office which puts people up — a kind of clearing house for traveling weirdos. They found me a room with a student in one of the dorms. He was in a wheelchair and had no motor control at all, but he was going to college. I could barely understand the guy. But he was really nice and let me use the floor in his room.

Anyway, I washed up and was just sitting there, since I couldn't carry on a conversation with the guy, when two other guys came up who took care of him. (They would take him to his classes and bring him back, wheel him to dinner, and all that.) They asked if I wanted to come to their room and listen to their new Seals and Crofts album. 'Hey, Seals and Crofts! Great!' I had their 'Year of Sunday' album. I used to listen to it every day, and never heard a word of it. But I loved the music.

We were listening to the record, when one guy turned to me and said, 'You know that Seals and Crofts are Bahá'ís, don't you?'

'Oh, that's neat.' (Every day I'm praying, 'God, please guide me! Show me the return of Christ!')

118

Then he said, 'We're Bahá'ís, too.'

'Oh, that's nice. I've got a book this girl just gave me.' And I told them about it. They didn't say a word. God bless those guys! They just said they were Bahá'ís. We spent the evening small-talking, and one of them invited me to breakfast the next morning, as he had an extra meal ticket.

So we went to breakfast. We sat and talked for an hour and a half about my search for the return of Christ. I told him that Christ had returned or He was going to return, and that all the Books were telling the same Truth. He just sat there and nodded his head, and was very loving. He never once said anything. The patience! How many of us could hold back and not say anything? And thank God! 'Cause if he had said something, he'd have blown it. When it was time to go, he just looked me in the eye and said, 'I hope you find what you're looking for.'

So I left Madison and started hitchhiking. I remember getting one ride that took me about fifteen miles. That was a big ride! The guy dropped me off on a dirt road in the middle of absolutely nowhere. There wasn't even a building that I could see. I said, 'Oh, God! I'm so tired! I've been traveling for months. Could you get me a ride to California!' A minute later, a guy pulled up in a Volkswagen and drove me to my parents' door.

As we were driving through Texas, he didn't feel like talking and I was a little tired of reading the New Testament, so I reached into my pack, way down at the bottom, and pulled out the book — *Thief in the Night: The Case of the Missing Millennium,* by William Sears. I started reading it. And I'm reading it, and I'm reading it, and my eyes are getting like saucers! By the fifteenth page, I knew I was onto it! I was devastated! I read the book from start to finish in about two and a half hours without taking a breath, or blinking. I had found what I was looking for.

119

I closed the book. I put it down. And I sat there. After an hour, I turned to the driver and said, 'I just read the most incredible book of my life!' I sat without moving for the rest of the day. I was stunned.

The next day I started getting a little angry. Who is this guy, Bill Sears? How do I know that he didn't fabricate the whole story? Right? The day before, I was convinced that I had found everything I was looking for. Now I wasn't so sure. But I had to find out.

When I got to my parents' home in Palm Springs, I went downtown to the bookstore. 'Hey! Do you have any books about the Bahá'í Faith?'

'No,' the guy behing the counter said, 'but there's a man in town named Tom, and he has lots of Bahá'í books.'

'What's his last name?'

'I don't know.'

'Where does he live?'

'I don't know where he lives.'

'Well, do you know where he works?'

'Look, man, all I know is the guy comes here once in a while. His name's Tom, and he's got Bahá'í books. What do you want from me?'

'Thanks, you've been a big help!

So I went to the library, and they had Bahá'í books. There were two more books by Bill Sears: *Wine of Astonishment* and *Release the Sun.* So I took 'em. They also had *Some Answered Questions* and *The Proclamation of Bahá'u'lláh.* I took all four of them, and buried myself in my room at my parents' house. Two days later I emerged. 'Here I am! What do they look like? Do I have to buy an earring?'

I didn't know who the Bahá'ís were or where to look for them. But I knew I was a Bahá'í. (I never once thought to check the phone book.) Every day I kept re-reading those books, devouring them, one after the other. And I started searching for Bahá'ís everywhere I went. I was on the look-out for any weird person. A month went by, and I didn't find any Bahá'ís.

Meanwhile, I had this motorcycle. A 1972 Harley Davidson, jet-black motorcycle. you know, the big one, with the sportster front end. I also had a full beard, hair down to my shoulders, and I used to wear a Castro hat. When I'd pull up to stoplights, parents would roll up the car windows and stuff their kids down on the floor — 'Hide, kids, hide!' And I'm just on my motorcycle, right?

Well, I didn't have a dime to my name. I was tired of living off my parents (they were probably more tired of it than I was), and I needed some cash. This motorcycle wasn't doing me any good. I didn't want to deal with motorcycles any more. So I put an ad in the paper to sell the thing, figuring I'd ask $2000 and the first one with $1500 could buy himself a bike. The ad ran four days. Not one call. Nobody. I couldn't believe it. On the fifth day, a guy called. We agreed to meet at my father's store, and I showed him the motorcycle. He mentioned that he'd just come back to the States from Argentina, and didn't have very much money. How much would I take for the bike? I told him $2000. 'All I've got's $1500,' he said. 'Take it or leave it.' I took the money.

The next day we went to change the paperwork at the Department of Motor Vehicles. While he was inside, I was waiting outside on my jet-black Harley Davidson motor-cycle, with my black leather jacket, and my Castro hat, and my beard, and my hair down to my shoulders. Sitting next to me in her car was this lovely woman who was the guy's wife. Typical, straight, middle class. I turned to her: 'Hey! Your husband was telling me that you were in Argentina. I used to live in Spain. How come you were in Argentina?

121

'Well,' she said, 'we were pioneers for the Bahá'í Faith.' My mouth dropped down to the second cylinder. I couldn't believe it!

'You were *what*!! I've been looking for Bahá'ís! I just read *Release the Sun*! I know all about Quddús and Mullá Husayn, the Báb and Bahá'u'lláh! And . . . and . . . *I'm* a Bahá'í!' *Her* mouth fell down, to the second cylinder. *She* couldn't believe it!

'Uh, there's a Bahá'í meeting tonight,' she said, 'but I'm not sure if it's open to non-Bahá'ís. Would you call me in an hour, and I'll let you know if you can come?' I called her back and she gave me the address. I knew I was going to a special event. So I took off my black leather jacket and my Castro hat, combed my hair, and dressed up in my nicest jeans. I didn't own the motorcycle any more, so I borrowed my parents' car and drove over to the house.

I knocked on the door. This wonderful-looking guy opened it and said, 'Hi! My name's Tom. I'm the librarian.' He took my hand. 'I'd like you to come in and meet our speaker tonight, Mr William Sears.' Mr. Sears *lived* in Palm Springs! He had just come back from Persia, and that night he showed the slides he had taken of the Bahá'í holy places. '. . . And this is where Quddús was martyred, and this . . .' All those pictures!

I spent several days with Tom, and every day I'd ask: 'Tom, how do you become a Bahá'í?' And he'd explain. Finally, after a week I said, 'Tom! *I* want to become a Bahá'í!' And so I did.

A Violin Alone

by Jeanne Janus

We came from Europe in 1950 to Ipswich, Massachusetts. One day, my husband's co-worker invited us to a fireside and we discovered that we had been Bahá'ís all along, without knowing it. However, we didn't want to belong to any religious organization. We felt we could just teach the Faith on our own.

A few weeks passed, during which we tried to give the Message of Bahá'u'lláh. After that, we attended another Bahá'í meeting. The speaker was astonished that we were Bahá'ís, but didn't want to sign an enrollment card. When we explained, he replied, 'If you are a violin, alone, you can play a tune. Together, you can play a symphony.' And that day we signed.

Alaskan Flashback

by Don Van Brunt

All I remember about the newspaper ad was that it was very small and announced a meeting that appeared to be about religion, 'at 8 p.m. on Tuesday, April 7, at the Dugout'. I clearly recall tossing the thought aside with, 'Who wants to go to a religious meeting?'

Since I worked the graveyard shift at the Ketchikan Pulp Mill, I was sleeping at 7.45 p.m., when suddenly I jumped out of the sack, threw on my clothes, ran down the stairs and sloshed rapidly through a heavy rain to get the American Legion Dugout by 8 o'clock — for a religious meeting.

'What?!' Halfway across the street I stopped. 'What in the heck's the matter with you, Van Brunt? You're nuts!' I went back to the curb and leaned on a wet pole. 'Nuts, and wide awake, and wet. Go back home, stupid, you've got three more hours to sleep!'

After seventeen years of searching and praying to God for 'understanding' and to know 'the purpose for my being', I never suspected that the answer to it all was just a couple of blocks up the street. I was still fighting the guidance for which I had so long and fervently prayed. As I leaned against that soggy pole, thoughts flashed through my mind. How long I stood there I don't know. I was way back along the trail of years:

FLASH — 1948: A trip from Grand Junction, Colorado, to San Francisco, California, to investigate 'Mental Physics'. Listened to the founder of this philosophy speak, completely discrediting his scheme in my eyes. Left with no further contact.

FLASH — 1957: 3 a.m. on a winding coastal road from Seattle to Fresno, doing 90 m.p.h. plus, sharp curve sign coming up, kept foot on pedal. 'Oh God! I'd just as soon it'd be now.' But my time was not up yet; the road stayed beneath me.

FLASH — December 1958: Santa Cruz, California. Gave away clothes, books, possessions. Sold car. Turned down good sign-painting job. Tried to find way to ship out to India to search Vedanta (Hindu) at its source. No jobs on ships. San Francisco, same thing. No jobs on ships. Seattle, same thing. Seamen in Union Hall with no work. No chance. Had about $85, and was wearing everything else I

124

owned. No rain gear and no winter clothing at all.

FLASH — Pan Am ticket office, Seattle. Sign in window: 'Alaska $66.00'. Bought ticket. Arrived Ketchikan with $6.75 on December 16, 1958, just before Christmas. No jobs. No one knew of any job possibilities. 'Do you have any kind of work for me?' Next place: 'Do you know any-one who needs help with anything?' Next afternoon: 'Yes, how would you like to clean out our warehouse?'

From the bottom it is clear that the only way one can go is UP. You can guess that I went to that meeting. You can be sure that a strong Hand pulled me to it. Bill DeForge, dynamic Auxiliary Board member, spoke about the Bahá'í Faith. I read all the pamphlets that were given to me, and there was never a doubt that I had found the Source of answers to all possible problems. A new world had opened up — from a state of chronic 'don't-give-a-damn-itis' to a state of unquestioned sureness, immediate and complete.

It had been a long search, with almost instant recognition at the last, and complete blindness until the moment that the final veil was lifted. The next evening I inquired as to how I might join the Bahá'í community. My enrollment card bears a June 4 date, but the important date for me is April 7 — when I discovered my religion had a name.

EPILOGUE — 1959 to present: Life began at age forty-five. The overflowing bounties of Bahá'u'lláh: summer schools; winter workshops; Yukon conferences; Kenai Institute; Local and National Assembly meetings; fair booths; speaking engagements; children's classes; custodian of first National Office, in Anchorage; pilgrimage to the Holy Land; teaching trips in Alaska, Canada, United States, Mexico, Central America; World Congress in London, 1963; dedication of the Bahá'í House of Worship in Panama, 1972; pioneering to Iceland,

1971-1975; Bahá'í marriage; loving friends; guest book full of names, memories; showers of material blessings; and most of all, the thrill of helping other souls to find this great gift of God.

Seize the Time

by Anne Gordon Atkinson

Seize the time, therefore, ere the glory of the divine springtime hath spent itself, and the Bird of Eternity ceased to warble its melody, that thy inner hearing may not be deprived of hearkening unto its call. This is My counsel unto thee and unto the beloved of God.

Bahá'u'lláh

I have often wondered if, at the hour of death, I will be able to say, 'Yes, I seized the time, Lord', or will find myself deprived of the immortal Beauty. The choice between oneness and separation has been a constant battle in my life; periods of inner knowing, joy, awe, and wonder have always been followed by times of doubt, despair, and self-search. The cycles show there is a difference, and the difference is largely one of choice, not accident or fate.

As a child I was intrigued by the notion of a God in the Presbyterian Church. Little of what the grown-ups said about this God ever made much sense to me. I assumed (because our church was very tall and was undergoing construction work within the sanctuary) that 'He' was some sort of Supreme Beam Support we visited on Sundays. This was the time of the popular 'God is dead' rumor. It frightened me to see those words printed across a record jacket, and to hear them on the lips of adults at parties. One morning, I climbed up the scaffolding inside the church to find out if what was up there had died. A workman discovered me, peacefully having a talk with the ceiling.

We lived in Little Rock, and I was only six when the high schools closed down because of the '58 race riots. Sometimes I would answer the phone and hear someone shriek 'nigger lovers!' then hang up. My mother would cry when I asked what it meant. One Sunday we took a house guest, a student from Africa, to church with us, and part of the congregation got up and walked out. Another part left when my father and Preacher Dick marched in Selma. Mother, who was serving on the school board, presented integration possibilities, but was defeated in the next election. It was a difficult time to be growing up in Arkansas.

I lived largely in a fantasy world of my own making. My ambitions were threefold: to become a writer, an actress, and a 'doctor of souls'. I imagined myself in the jungles of Africa, healing people with miracles, words, and performances. I imitated book and film heroines, constantly wore costumes, and had great dialogues with imaginary friends in the privacy of a playhouse or closet. I played 'prisoner', writing of my sufferings to the outside world in a secret code I had invented.

One of my favorite friends was a ballerina doll from New York, who I knew would come alive if I prayed hard enough and left food out for her. Each morning before leaving for school, I carefully instructed my mother what to give her for lunch. Apparently Mother forgot to feed the poor thing, and my interests gradually shifted to learning how to fly. I resolutely consulted God about this wish, and practised jumping from the back of the couch while flapping my arms wildly. In dreams and in my own mind, I flew.

127

I was blessed with secret powers and amazed my imaginary friends.

The Civil War period intrigued me. I ardently read all the books I could about it, wrote stories about characters of that time, dressed in costume, and put the date '1863' on all my school papers.

I finally found a friend to join me in my fantasy world, and together, in old-fashioned clothes, we pretended to be the twin incarnations of the returned Christ. Imaginary enemies threw stones at us while we jumped on her trampoline, talking of our teachings for the world. But our families went to different chuches. Her God wanted hats and kneeling benches, while I could gaze, hatless, up at mine. We gradually drifted apart.

At thirteen, I sadly accepted the disappearance of my childhood and wrote in my diary,

> All I have now is a head full of memories ... My goal is to grow into a mature adult, sensible, intelligent, and honest. I'll still join in fun and activities, but all the while be searching, searching, searching for something I cannot yet grasp.
>
> (September 1965)

I thought I had lost the magic and certainty of my childhood. I prayed that God would release me from this world and take me to a planet which knew no crime, no racial animosity, no modern invention, and no growing up. I wanted the time-set to be 1863. I waited.

One night, at a Young Life Christian retreat in Colorado, I experienced a 'revelation' and accepted anew the inner light that I thought was extinguished. My friends rejoiced that I had been born again. At home, Bible study groups were organized and we had a tight-knit circle of friends through Christ.

But it did not last long for me. I rebelled against conservatism, began reading Sartre, Camus, and Dostoevsky, and dropped out of Young Life meetings. My friends prayed for me, in hopes that Satan would stop whispering in my ear. I was introduced to hallucinogenic experiences, new music, new ideas. A group of us wore black armbands against the Viet Nam war. I plunged into existential despair, the dark night of the soul. It lasted one year.

During that time, I was hospitalized with the rare and often fatal Rocky Mountain spotted fever. In my delirium, and to the doctors' amazement, I diagnosed the disease and willed myself to recovery. I had had a glimpse of the other world, and was not yet ready for it.

One week later, I flew away to college in Massachusetts. There my thoughts turned inwards. 'I look at the reflection of the white birch in the pond', I wrote, inspired by Emerson,

> and suddenly see an image more real than the tree above it; the reflection moves, it breathes, it grows, it fluctuates, it reaches out and withdraws, it gives. This is surely the essence of the tree itself, yet the real tree has a cold, almost lifeless appearance in comparison! Similarly, I lean over the bridge to seek my own image and find it as unrecognizable. Gazing intently at the shadowy picture, I see a living form, almost as if struggling to be freed from a restricting force. From my limited perceptions, I see that this image has great capabilities; it can think, it can act and remember, it can take a moment in time and live in it. How remarkable! As I look even closer, I see something of a divine nature in the moving image. It seems to say, 'If I can define myself, I can understand the universe and its creator because I am a fraction of both.' I feel a certain

reverence towards the living creature; little of his worth is ever really recognized, yet it seems he is continuously striving. The water becomes smooth and I see myself . . .

(November 1970)

Yet doubts plagued my world.

Everything is paradoxical . . . What happens to a nine-teen-year-old girl when life has embittered her, when her innocence and youth are gone, when she is surrounded only by an empty shell? A ghost is left that feels no mirth, none of the bubbly joy of living that it once knew, but only sorrow and anguish . . . Where am I going? Is there no one to squeeze my shaking hand? I have no one. I am a loner, with the soul of a haunted artist; a poet whose feelings cannot be turned into words. The life I have chosen is necessarily godless — my faith must lie in myself alone. I must walk hand in hand with the dictates of my own soul. Which voice out of thousands inside of me will I listen to? Which song will I sing? Why must life be so painful?

(February and April 1971)

That spring I began studying dreams and was obsessed by modern religious literature. In one dream, I was discussing dreams with my religion professor. 'Dr Forman,' I asked, 'does the search for salvation occur throughout your dreams?' I never got an answer about *his* search for salvation. Obviously, I was questioning mine.

A group of us went to Washington, DC, to participate in the huge May Day moratorium against the war in Viet Nam. We went down in caravan, passing pipes, food, songs, and hopes for the future between cars *en route*. We were going with a singleness of purpose, with hopeful idealism. To many of us, the days there were devastating. No one listened to our pleas for peace. I fasted, slept on church pews, withdrew with conviction from the world of drugs and rock music, sought my own inner calm. I returned, disillusioned, vowing to embrace other solutions, other creeds.

At the end of the school year, I found myself at a Catholic retreat called the 'House of Prayer' in Gloucester, Massachusetts. There, sunrise chanting, hatha yoga, meditation, work in silence, and a meatless diet became part of my everyday reality. In the afternoons, I spent hours out on the rocky shore, asking questions aloud of the universe until I became hoarse. Only the rhythm of the sea responded; there were seemingly no answers. I wrote:

> god
> where are you?
> do you seek me as i seek you?
> (am i as well concealed?)
> i want this to be a two-way thing, lord,
> but i don't know where to start.
> if you are dead, how can i believe?
> if you are alive, why can't i believe?
> am i destined to become a
> god-forsaken cain,
> believing only in myself?
> if i am real to me
> why can't you be real as well?
> do you hear my questions, lord?
> or is it only a meaningless void
> that receives them in silence?
> where are you?
> god?

(May 1971)

131

One day a woman of middle age appeared, wearing a blue muslin tunic. Her grey hair tumbled over her shoulders, and her countenance was of a radiance I had never seen before. I was serving lunch to the nuns and monks when she arrived, and nearly dropped the tray I carried. During the meal I was spellbound, enamoured of her eloquence. After the others had left the table, I found myself kneeling at the feet of our honored guest. 'Ellafern,' I asked her, 'What is faith in God?' She stroked my hair. 'I love you, child,' was her only answer.

That night we went next door to a session of meditation at a yoga retreat. The Indian guru asked Ellafern to divulge to the group the truths she had obviously found. I waited proudly for the eloquent tongue to speak. She simply lowered her head and replied in a whisper, 'It's all in the Lord.'

What did *that* mean? I was furious at not knowing and decided to go with her to her farm in Virginia in order to glean from her wisdom. We made it as far as the Integral Yoga Institute in New York City. I went walking in the city and came back, in turmoil. 'Child, child, the way is narrow and hard,' she said to me, aware of my distress. 'You are not ready to leave behind your playthings and follow an austere path. I must leave you here, now. If you need me in the future, you will find me. You have your own faith to find and to follow.' Then she was gone.

Alone, I knew calm and and a new kind of love. I knew too, perhaps for the first time, the 'peace that passeth understanding'. I was no longer afraid to believe; I had entered a new garden.

When I returned to the van we had come in, I found that my possessions had been stolen — guitar, camera, a few clothes — but I was not upset. How meaningless they now seemed compared to my new treasures, inner ones, as well as things I had collected along the beach, and an Indian shawl of Ellafern's. The shawl was hand woven, very clean, and delicate. I took it as if it were a gift I was unworthy of — something to remind me of her radiance and love.

Before heading home, I stopped in Philadelphia and met a friend who took me to see the Amish people. Another side trip was to an immense Pentacostal gathering where people spoke in tongues and prophesied. I left perplexed about religion. Was there no universal pathway which would include all human thought, modes of dress, cultures, and temperaments? My curiosity could not be contained. I flew home and enrolled in a comparative religions course.

I became immersed in the study of religion, almost to the exclusion of all else. Each morning my preparation included rising long before dawn, meditating before a homemade altar with Ellafern's shawl on it, driving up a nearby mountain for sunrise chanting and hatha yoga, and arriving early before class began, to read from the scriptures under the pine trees. To the surprise and bewilderment of my friends and parents, I became a strict vegetarian and practiced 'ahimsa', the doctrine of non-violence to any living thing.

One morning when I was particularly inspired, a stranger approached, having noticed my habitual sitting beneath a certain tree. 'Watcha doin'?' he asked casually. 'I'm practicing a yoga posture,' I explained. 'Well, ah've heard of yoghurt, but what in the heck is yeoga?' There were others who were puzzled by my behavior in that summer of '71.

In recurrent dreams, I would be confused about directions, possessions would be stolen, and a beautiful child would appear in ruins, as if to guide me. In one dream, I kept going up and down various flights of stairs and enter-

133

ing different rooms. I finally ran into a priest and asked him how I could get to Main Street. He told me to go through another room, out the door, and across the meadow. From there I would have to find it myself. A bus was going, but I knew I should choose and follow my own way.

One day after class, when my instructor passed me under the pine trees, I caught up with him and asked, 'Dr Slinkard, what do *you* think faith in God is?' He replied with the following story:

> A man was watching another prepare to walk across a rope stretched over Niagara Falls, with a wheelbarrow balanced in front of him. 'Do you believe I can make it?' the performer asked the man watching. 'Sure I do,' replied the other confidently. 'Then get in!' said the first, gesturing toward the wheelbarrow.

My instructor then nodded and left abruptly.

One evening at a swimming party, a group of friends asked what I had been doing. Feeling that by now I was quite an authority on the world's religions (after all, I had been ardently making comparisons for three weeks), I launched into a discourse about wonders of Krishna, Lao-tzu, Buddha, Zoroaster, Guru Nanak, Muḥammad, and Christ, and the similarities of their lives and teachings. 'Have you heard of Bahá'u'lláh, the Bahá'í prophet?' a young man asked me. I chose to ignore the question, thinking he was referring to some new sect or cult. He kept following me around the swimming pool, trying to tell me of the Message he had recently heard. I thought he was nuts. Surely I *knew* about all of the existing authentic religions. He apparently had met a Bahá'í one evening and had talked to him until dawn. He was inspired, but confused about the facts. Finally, I agreed to read a book the

Bahá'í had given him.

That week, I dreamed of an eastern temple with camels and tall trees surrounding it. It was like a mosque, only more modern, and very vivid to me. Then I was with a professor and another student. There were five or six books in front of us, with eastern titles. They had been written recently. The student asked if I had read them, and I replied that I had only read Hesse's books on the East. Then I was riding a bicycle down a long highway. I met a boy who asked me questions about Ultimate Reality, God, Being, etc. I told him to follow me. The power went out of my bicycle and I coasted to a place where the road divided in two. The lower road was very easy to get onto; the higher one was a continuation of the first, though rougher and harder to stay on. I chose it. My bicycle began working again. I came to a Romanesque, white-columned platform with a roof. There were many steps in front of it, and I rode up them on my bike. At the top there were some women running a dancing school. I asked them which way I should go. One responded, 'Choose your own way.' I was perplexed and impatient.

It was a week before I had time to look at *Bahá'í World Faith*. I felt my other studies were more important. But I distinctly remember picking up the red volume, opening it to a passage, reading one paragraph by Bahá'u'lláh, closing the book in absolute amazement, and pacing back and forth. It was too powerful to have been written by a person. I was suddenly overwhelmed with fear and excitement. Either this was something I shouldn't delve into, or it was the key to connecting everything! I called up the young man I had met at the party. 'Frank, please come over here right now!' I asked him question after question, and he told me what little he knew about the Bahá'í Faith.

I had to know more. But I remembered being curious as

135

a child about Joseph Smith and Mormonism, then being disappointed when I found out more about it. Would this, too, disappoint me?

Frank suggested that we try to locate some Bahá'ís to talk to. 'In Little Rock?' I laughed. 'The closest place they'd probably be is Memphis or St. Louis.' We found a listing in the phone book. I was half afraid to call, thinking they'd try to pull us into their secret cult. I made Frank hold my hand while the phone was ringing. Who knows what would answer at the other end? A woman's voice. I asked if we could find out something about Bahá'í. She introduced herself and said there was a fireside that evening. Would we like to come? I hesitated. What kind of strange ritual would we be getting ourselves into? I said yes, not sure of anything but my sweating palms.

We were the first to arrive. Two teenage girls (one black, one white) were giggling as they answered the door. 'How dare they laugh, while we have come searching for truth!' I thought. There was no incense, no strange altar, no pews or pillows in sight. It was a normal living room. The father of one of the girls walked in. We sat on the floor and he joined us. 'What questions do you have?' he asked, noticing we had a book. I blurted out a dozen or so in the first two minutes. He smiled, and began one by one to explain, speaking with a directness that went right to the heart, yet through the mind in a way I had always yearned for. My insides trembled, weeping and dancing and turning a thousand cartwheels. 'But what about . . .' I would interject when a new point was brought up. Again the calm directness. Answers falling upon my ears. Answers! Had I not always waited for these answers? I felt like doubting Thomas, but continued my questions. Each was met with a viable, honest-to-goodness answer. Finally I sat back, stunned. I had nothing more to say.

That night had changed my life, though it was a long time before I realized just how much. Little by little I incorporated my Bahá'í studies into my other studies, telling everyone I saw about my new findings. With my professor's permission, I invited two Bahá'í speakers to address my class one day. Many of the students were impressed and several attended firesides. I wrote a paper comparing yoga, the Jesus Movement, the Zen experience of *satori*, and the Bahá'í Faith, expressing amazement at the diversity of man's beliefs and practices. 'But greater than this amazement', I wrote,

> has been the realization that the truths underlying the outward manifestations of religion are essentially the same; throughout history some eternal Something (be it Allah, Krishna, Ahura Mazda, or God) has continuously delivered to man its essence in the words suited to man at that place and that time.

I voiced limitations in both the 'Jesus Revolution' and the life set up by serious yoga adherents.

> Though these sects have brought a great deal of peace and joy to their members, they offer little elasticity (i.e., they are not tolerant in the sense of true religion their demands cannot be met by all, and thus they are exclusive organizations, somewhat dependent upon environment for a conducive atmosphere).

I went on to talk about the Bahá'í Faith, contrasting it with the others:

> Several weeks ago I stumbled upon the Bahá'í Faith, which interested me at first from a purely intellectual stand point. Their explanation for the sudden

137

spiritual awakening throughout the world is more fantastic, while at the same time more advanced and feasible than most: the outpouring of the Holy Spirit through the latest 'Manifestation of God', the Prophet Bahá'u'lláh, has influenced the lives of all and inspires receptive minds even in places and among peoples where the name of the Prophet is quite unknown. Bahá'u'lláh himself says of his era: 'Is not the object of every Revelation to effect a transformation in the whole character of mankind, a transformation that shall manifest itself both outwardly and inwardly, that shall affect both its inner life and external conditions? For if the character of mankind be not changed, the futility of God's universal Manifestations would be apparent.'

And I quoted 'Abdu'l-Bahá's definition, 'To be a Bahá'í simply means to love all the world; to love humanity and try to serve it; to work for universal peace and universal brotherhood.' The paper was given an A.

I, however, was still a little uncertain. I believed in Bahá'u'lláh and never questioned His authority; I knew that this religion was the most advanced one on the planet; I knew that Bahá'í (which means 'follower of the Light') was the highest path one could tread. Yet something in me hesitated to join. I saw the Bahá'ís as much too social, much too happy. I was not ready to emerge from my contemplative state to accept a social order.

One night in August I had the following dream:

I was wandering through a hospital, trying to find a room to stay in. I kept going up and down the elevator, looking in various rooms. I learned that I was going to have to be put to death by submersion in water. I thought at first that I would have to jump from a high roof in order to destroy my physical self in the pool. This was not the case. As I went towards the pool, I saw two Bahá'ís holding covered platters with the heads of my sister and myself on them, preparing to submerge them. We watched while our heads were submerged. Suddenly, I saw life through new eyes, sensed the futility of earthly existence, and vowed to make the best of my last days here. I walked off, ghost-like, translucent, and found my boyfriend, Jeff, sitting under some pine trees, drinking. He muttered something to me, then walked off with someone else. To no one could I communicate the feelings of my death/rebirth.

(23 August 1971)

This symbolic baptism by the Bahá'ís seemed to represent a change in my subconscious awareness. I became focused on this world as preparation for a next one, as one stage before another. Religion became progressive, not stagnant or lifeless.

The next night I went to a fireside at the home of a blind couple, whose insights amazed me. An old childhood friend was there. Mary and I had grown up as next door neighbors. We had gone in radically opposite directions for a few years, and were now re-meeting at firesides. She had become a Bahá'í upon hearing William Sears speak at the Bahá'í House of Worship in Wilmette, Illinois.

The speaker finished his presentation, then asked if there were questions. I had one. 'How does one rid oneself from the obscuring dust of all acquired knowledge and the allusions of the embodiments of satanic fancy?' I had been studying a passage known as the 'Tablet of the True Seeker' from Bahá'u'lláh's *Kitáb-i-Íqán*. It was a question I had been worrying over for days.

I do not recall the discussion that followed. In the middle of it someone asked me, 'Why aren't you a Bahá'í?' I replied, a little sadly, that I could not love all the world. 'Oh, yes you can! And you do,' another Bahá'í reassured me. I (the little 'I' that had to die in the dream) was defeated. 'All right, then pass me a declaration card.' I felt resigned. At once there was a great clapping and commotion. People were hugging me and welcoming me into the family. I was a bit stunned. What step had I taken?

That night I couldn't sleep from excitement. A secret, inner recognition began to grow upon declaring, upon yielding the smaller self to something larger. Life has never been the same since. Now, almost fourteen years later, I ask what has constituted the difference.

A world of experiences rises up in the mind — experiences it would take volumes to recount — that have led to Panama, Ireland, Canada, Israel, all across America, and the Caribbean. Everywhere, friends. Everywhere, the growing evidence of a new world order beginning to flower. I see the earth as my home and can't imagine not having the ties that come automatically to one who has believed in Bahá'u'lláh. Of course there are still personal tests, moments of anger, grief, and doubt. But they fade to nothingness when one returns to the Light.

At my first Bahá'í conference, in Reno, Nevada, I saw a slide show of the Master in America.

> His face, with the sunken eyes and gentle lines caused by a lifetime of suffering, seemed so kind, so forgiving, yet so very strong and compelling. The final slide was a full length view of 'Abdu'l-Bahá standing with a rose in His hand, and the words, 'I am waiting. I am patiently waiting.' Tears fell freely onto my cheeks as it struck me that in spite of the slowness and awkward-

ness of humanity, those souls who are born of God never give up; they await our reconciliation with the utmost compassion and mercy. Silence. Then from an old squeaky tape came the Master's voice, chanting. It caused a deep stirring in my soul, and again, tears fell without notice. I sat in awed contemplation. The lights went up, the audience began greeting each other. As I looked at the many radiant faces, it was as though they had merged into one. Speechless, I wandered, seeing the believers with new eyes, as though they were in reality flawless and harmonious beings, a new race of men. The beauty of the Beloved I saw on each one's face. This was Bahá'u'lláh's promise fulfilled! We are the new race of men He spoke of, united, trusting, radiant with hope and confident of the future.

(April 1972)

That night, wearing the shawl that once draped my altar, I was walking home through the streets of Reno with my new Bahá'í friend Monica. I told her my story. When she asked my first mentor's name, we stopped. 'Ellafern!' we both cried in the same breath. She had had the same experience with her in Virginia that I'd had in Massachusetts. Both of us had been drawn to follow her, but had been turned away to become Bahá'ís!

Back at Mills College, a friend named Carla came to visit my room one night. She poured her woes into my hands. It was the first time anyone had ever done that. I got out the shawl and draped it around her, knowing it was time to pass it on. 'I love you, child,' was all I could say. Carla became a Bahá'í the next fall.

In Panama, I recorded the following:

Slowly, I open my eyes to the new day. It is 6.00 a.m. and already the sun is quite high. From my top bunk I have a view of the lush tropical landscape, and of the newly dedicated Bahá'í temple, gleaming in its whiteness, from a faraway hillside. The music from a soft Spanish guitar filters in from the porch, and by now I can recognize words of the song, such as 'unity' and 'mankind'. Next to me, my Venezuelan and Black American friends are still sleeping in their bunks. All of the Indian women have been up for some time, washing out their colorful clothes and hanging them in the sun to dry. One of them brings a bright green lovebird perched on her finger to my bedside. 'Willy', she says, and croons to him. I laughingly share a sink with an elderly lady from Australia, and try a few words of Spanish with a small Peruvian girl. Outdoors, I join my Persian and Japanese friends for morning prayers and meditations. We get into a heavy conversation about the concept of justice for the new age, which is interrupted by a charming lad from Colombia who wants to teach us a new song. After breakfast, too many of us pile into an old school bus marked 'Istituto Bahá'í', but no one complains of discomfort; we are too busy singing and waving at other friends we pass along the way. At the conference center, we join several hundred others of our world family. Workshops begin on many subjects, but some of us opt to go out to teach the people of Panama. Everyone wants to know. They are wondering about the strange new building up on the hillside. Many questions are asked of us, and eyes invariably light up. 'Can I too be a Bahá'í?' They have no diffi-

142

culty accepting the station of Bahá'u'lláh. Our hearts overflow with love for our new family members.

(April 1972)

This was only the prelude to my new life as a Bahá'í. Experience had confirmed what I had read in the Writings, those vast marvels of scripture written for our times. Had I neglected to heed them, had I refused the book or not attended that first fireside, I would have been deprived of all the richness of subsequent experience.

Some say that once having found, one can easily become complacent, and then outgrow the finding. But on this pathway, there is the constant challenge to renew oneself in the immensity of the Revelation, to grow in maturity and heroism as the world suffers the birth pangs of change, to 'seize the time' before the springtime is past, to offer the Counsel to those who would otherwise be deprived. How else will we attain the station of the 'beloved of God'?

Index of Authors